The 12-Week DIABETES Cookbook

Your Super Simple Plan for Organizing, Budgeting, and Cooking Amazing Dinners

LINDA GASSENHEIMER

Associate Publisher, Books, Abe Ogden; Managing Editor, Rebekah Renshaw; Acquisitions Editor, Victor Van Beuren; Editor, Lauren Wilson; Production Manager, Melissa Sprott; Composition, Melissa Sprott; Interior Design: pixiedesign, llc; 4/Color Food Photography, Mittera Group; Cover Design, pixiedesign, llc; Printer, Versa Press.

Printed in the United States of America
1 3 5 7 9 10 8 6 4 2

The suggestions and information contained in this publication are generally consistent with the *Standards of Medical Care in Diabetes* and other policies of the American Diabetes Association, but they do not represent the policy or position of the Association or any of its boards or committees. Reasonable steps have been taken to ensure the accuracy of the information presented. However, the American Diabetes Association cannot ensure the safety or efficacy of any product or service described in this publication. Individuals are advised to consult a physician or other appropriate health care professional before undertaking any diet or exercise program or taking any medication referred to in this publication. Professionals must use and apply their own professional judgment, experience, and training and should not rely solely on the information contained in this publication before prescribing any diet, exercise, or medication. The American Diabetes Association—its officers, directors, employees, volunteers, and members—assumes no responsibility or liability for personal or other injury, loss, or damage that may result from the suggestions or information in this publication.

♾ The paper in this publication meets the requirements of the ANSI Standard Z39.48-1992 (permanence of paper).

ADA titles may be purchased for business or promotional use or for special sales. To purchase more than 50 copies of this book at a discount, or for custom editions of this book with your logo, contact the American Diabetes Association at the address below or at booksales@diabetes.org.

American Diabetes Association
2451 Crystal Drive, Suite 900
Arlington, VA 22202

Library of Congress Cataloging-in-Publication Data
Names: Gassenheimer, Linda, author.
Title: The budget-conscious diabetes meal planner / Linda Gassenheimer.
Description: Arlington : American Diabetes Association, [2018]
Identifiers: LCCN 2017013400 | ISBN 9781580406765
Subjects: LCSH: Diabetes--Diet therapy--Recipes. | Low budget cooking. | LCGFT: Cookbooks.
Classification: LCC RC662 .G362 2018 | DDC 641.5/6314--dc23
LC record available at https://lccn.loc.gov/2017013400

DEDICATION

To my husband, Harold, for his love, constant enthusiasm for my work, and support.

TABLE OF **CONTENTS**

WEEK ELEVEN

WEEK TWELVE

ACKNOWLEDGMENTS

One of the best parts of writing a book is working with so many talented and friendly people. I'd like to thank them all for their enthusiastic support.

My biggest thank you goes to my husband, Harold, who encouraged me, helped me test every recipe, and spent hours helping me edit every word. His constant encouragement for all of my work has made this book a partnership.

Another big thank you goes to the wonderful team at the American Diabetes Association. It's been a delight working with all of them.

Thank you to Abe Ogden, Associate Publisher, Books, at the American Diabetes Association, for his guidance and support.

To Rebekah Renshaw, Managing Editor, and Victor Van Beuren, Acquisitions Editor, at the American Diabetes Association: thank you for your advice and wonderful work in managing the book.

Lauren Wilson, Editor, thank you for helping to bring this book to life.

I'd, also like to thank my family members, who have always supported my projects and encouraged me every step of the way: James and Patty, and their children, Zach, Jacob, and Haley; John and Jill and their children, Jeffrey and Joanna; Charles and his sons, Daniel and Matthew; and my sister Roberta, and her husband, Robert.

And finally, thank you to all of my readers, listeners to my WLRN NPR program, and social media friends who have written and called over the years. You have helped shape my ideas and turned the solitary task of writing into a two-way street.

INTRODUCTION

Looking for a way to cut down on food shopping time and cost? Try these 12 weeks of quick and easy, family-friendly recipes.

With this plan, you can do your shopping for the week on one day and buy all the ingredients you need to make meals for the entire week. Buying the food you need, and nothing extra, will save you money.

The simple recipes in this book are packed with flavors you'll enjoy. Each night has a new taste—no eating the same leftovers again. You'll find a wide variety of exciting ethnic dishes as well as your favorite comfort foods.

Can I tempt you with a few of these dinners?

You can make a Crispy Chicken with Ratatouille, cooking enough chicken to enjoy a quick Crispy Chicken Sandwich supper on another night. If you buy enough ground buffalo for two meals, you'll enjoy a family-pleasing Spaghetti and Meatballs on one night and Southwestern Buffalo Sliders with Taco Salad on another.

You can make an Herb-Crusted Pork Tenderloin dinner and cook enough pork to fill a Barbecued Pork Sandwich on another night.

Feeling like a steak? You can cook enough steak to make Garlic Steak and Linguine with Shredded Carrots on one night and a Hot and Spicy Stir-Fry Beef with Sesame Noodles on another.

This book will help you get started on the quick, flavorful road to meal planning success.

SHOPPING LIST

Each of the 12 weeks of meals in this book is accompanied by a shopping list that contains not only all of the ingredients you'll need for the week, but also the amount you will need of each ingredient. That way, if you already have some of the ingredient on hand, you'll be able to tell if you have enough or need to buy more. This is especially helpful for spices and bottled sauces.

In addition, the shopping list is organized according to supermarket department. With large supermarkets, it can be annoying to realize that you forgot something in the dairy department when you're in the produce section. These lists should help, and may even cut down the amount of time you spend shopping.

RECIPES

The recipes for each week start on Sunday and are arranged by day for optimum freshness of the food bought. If you shop on a different day of the week, simply start with the first meal for the week on that day and continue in order. Each recipe has a Helpful Hints section to give you cooking and shopping tips. And there is a Countdown to help you know in what order to cook the food. All of the recipes in this book serve four.

WEEKLY BUDGET

Each meal in this book lists the cost per person and each week has an average cost per person for the seven dinners in the week. Some days may be more than the average, and others less. The average cost for the 12 weeks of dinners is just over $5.00 per person per day. The estimated prices of ingredients are based on national food store prices and will vary according to areas and seasons. These numbers will give you an idea of what you are spending on your meals. Also keep an eye out for sales when shopping for further cost savers.

TIPS FOR SHOPPING AND STORING INGREDIENTS

PRODUCE

Ask for large packages of fruits and vegetables to be broken down for you. Many stores will accommodate this request. If you have several vegetables left at the end of the week, think about making soup. It's easy. Here's a basic recipe: sauté the vegetables until tender, add chicken broth or water to cover the vegetables and simmer 20 minutes. Add any leftover fresh herbs for added flavor. Divide the soup into single portions and freeze for a quick lunch option.

CANNED GOODS

Freeze any extra canned tomatoes after opening, whether diced, whole, or in sauce form. Be sure to mark the amount and date on the container before freezing. I also freeze extra tomato purée.

EQUIPMENT

- **Kitchen Scale:** It's helpful to have a kitchen scale. This makes measuring your ingredients a breeze.
- **Skillets:** The recipes in this book make four servings. You will need a large skillet for many of these recipes. If you don't have one, use two smaller skillets.
- **Food Processor:** A food processor is a great tool for quickly chopping or mixing ingredients.
- **Baking Sheets**

SHOP SMART

Many products are now lower in sodium and sugar. To help you chose the right products, I give you the key nutritional information you need to look for on the labels. This Shop Smart guide isn't a specific recommendation of any particular brand. You can choose from the many options available. The key is to shop smart by looking at the nutritional information provided in this section and in the individual recipes. You may not find the exact values I suggest on the shelves of your grocery store, but you can use this information as a guideline for what you choose.

Look for:

SAUCES

Low-sodium, no-sugar-added pasta sauce containing per cup (8 ounces): 131 calories, 3.8 g fat, 20.7 g carbohydrate, 77 mg sodium.

Low-sodium tomato sauce containing per cup (8 ounces): 103 calories, 0.5 g fat, 21.3 g carbohydrate, 21 mg sodium.

Barbecue sauce containing per tablespoon: 28 calories, 6.5 g carbohydrate, 199 mg sodium.

Reduced-fat oil and vinegar dressing containing per tablespoon: 11 calories, 1.0 g fat, 4 mg sodium.

Low-sodium teriyaki sauce containing per tablespoon: 8 calories, 1.5 g carbohydrate, 168 mg sodium.

CANNED FOODS

Canned potatoes containing per cup: 112 calories, 0.36 g fat, 24.5 g carbohydrate, 24 mg sodium.

Low-sodium diced tomatoes containing per cup: 41 calories, 9.6 g carbohydrate, 24 mg sodium.

SPICE

Salt-free or low-sodium Cajun seasoning blend. McCormick Perfect Pinch Cajun Seasoning or The Spice Hunter salt-free Cajun Seasoning blend fit this profile.

MEAT

Lean ground veal containing per ounce: 43 calories, 2 g fat, 1 g saturated fat.

WEEK **ONE**

WEEKLY BUDGET
Average cost of a meal per person for the week is
$5.41

SUNDAY NIGHT
CRISPY CHICKEN WITH RATATOUILLE (SAUTÉED PROVENÇAL VEGETABLES).
Taste the flavors of Provence with crispy chicken and vegetables in a tomato sauce. Save some chicken for Tuesday night's meal.

MONDAY NIGHT
SPAGHETTI AND MEATBALLS
This is always a family favorite. It's made with ground buffalo that has a real beef flavor and is low in saturated fat.

TUESDAY NIGHT
CRISPY CHICKEN SANDWICH WITH SPICY COLESLAW
Make enough chicken on Sunday for a quick and easy Crispy Chicken Sandwich on Tuesday night.

WEDNESDAY NIGHT
SOUTHWESTERN BUFFALO SLIDERS WITH TACO SALAD
Savor the earthy flavors of the Southwest with sliders that use the remaining ground buffalo purchased for the week.

THURSDAY NIGHT
BAKED PARMESAN SCALLOPS WITH SPINACH LINGUINE AND CARROTS
A Parmesan topping coats the scallops in this dish, and the linguine is served in a delicious white wine sauce. Using frozen scallops means you can buy them on Sunday and they will be good to use on Thursday night and Saturday night.

FRIDAY NIGHT
ORZO AND THREE-CHEESE "RISOTTO" WITH TOMATO AND ONION SALAD
This creamy pasta dish served with a tomato salad makes a great vegetarian dinner.

SATURDAY NIGHT
THAI PEANUT AND COCONUT SCALLOPS WITH GINGER RICE
Finish your week with a spicy Thai dish and ginger-flavored rice.

SHOPPING LIST

SHOP SMART

- Look for low-sodium pasta sauce containing per 1/2 cup: 112 calories, 3.5 g fat, 17.7 g carbohydrate, 39 mg sodium.
- Look for low-sodium tomato sauce containing per cup (8 ounces): 103 calories, 0.5 g fat, 21.3 g carbohydrate, 21 mg sodium.
- Look for reduced-fat oil and vinegar dressing containing per tablespoon: 11 calories, 1.0 g fat, 4 mg sodium.

Here is the Shopping List for this week's dinners.

This shopping list will help you get in and out of the market quickly. The ingredients are listed by supermarket department to make shopping easier; you won't forget something in one department and have to go back and forth across the store.

The amount needed of each ingredient is listed so you will know what size package or can to buy. If it helps you to better visualize the amount you need, please note that 4 tablespoons equal 1/4 cup and 8 tablespoons equal 1/2 cup.

Make sure to check your refrigerator and pantry to see if you have any of these ingredients on hand before making your trip to the market.

MEAT AND SEAFOOD

3 pounds frozen sea scallops
3 pounds ground buffalo
3 pounds boneless, skinless chicken thighs

DAIRY

4 ounces crumbled feta cheese (2/3 cup needed)
1 small carton nonfat ricotta cheese (1/2 cup needed)
1 small piece Parmesan cheese (3/4 cup grated needed)
1 small bottle skim milk (1/4 cup needed)
1 small package butter (3 teaspoons needed)
1 container eggs (4 eggs needed)

BAKERY

8 whole-wheat slider rolls
1 small loaf whole-meal, multigrain country bread (5 slices needed)
4 whole-wheat kaiser rolls (3 ounces each)

CONDIMENTS

1 small bottle peanut sauce (4 tablespoons needed)
1 small can light coconut milk (3/4 cup needed)
1 small bottle reduced-fat mayonnaise (10 tablespoons needed)
1 small bottle distilled white vinegar (2 tablespoons needed)
1 jar Dijon mustard (1/2 tablespoon needed)
1 small box brown sugar (2 teaspoons needed)
1 small jar bread-and-butter pickles (1/4 cup needed)
1 bottle/can low-sodium pasta sauce (1 1/2 [12 ounces] cups needed) (see *Shop Smart*, opposite)
1 bottle low-sodium, no-sugar-added canned tomato sauce (3 cups [24 ounces] needed) (see *Shop Smart*, opposite)
1 container fat-free, no-salt-added chicken broth (4 cups needed)

SPICE SECTION

1 small bottle ground ginger (3 teaspoons needed)
1 small bottle cayenne pepper (1/2 teaspoon needed)
1 bottle chipotle powder (2 teaspoons needed)
1 small container saffron (1 teaspoon needed)
1 small bottle ground sage (2 teaspoons needed)
1 bottle dried oregano (if not using fresh oregano)

PASTA, RICE, BREAD CRUMBS, CHIPS

Microwaveable brown basmati rice (to make 3 cups cooked rice)
1 box orzo (2 cups needed)
8 ounces fresh spinach linguine or 6 ounces dried linguine
1/2 pound whole-wheat spaghetti
1 small package cornmeal (1/2 cup needed)
1 package low-fat baked tortilla chips (3 cups needed)
1 package whole-wheat plain bread crumbs (1/2 cup needed)

ALCOHOL AND WINE

1 small bottle white wine (1 1/4 cups needed)

PRODUCE

1 bag washed, ready-to-eat spinach (8 cups needed)
3 large onions (6 cups needed)
1 red onion (1 1/4 cups needed)
2 red bell peppers (2 cups needed)
2 bags washed, ready-to-eat shredded iceberg lettuce (16 cups needed)
1 bag washed, ready-to-eat romaine lettuce, cut into bite-size pieces (6 cups needed)
4 tomatoes (4 cups needed)
1 bunch fresh parsley (1/2 cup needed)
1 bunch fresh oregano (1/4 cup needed)
1 package sliced carrots (1 cup needed)
1 pound eggplant
1 pound zucchini
1/2 pound sliced button mushrooms
1 package washed, ready-to-eat shredded cabbage (4 cups needed)

STAPLES

Canola oil
Olive oil
Olive oil spray
Garlic (8 cloves needed)
Reduced-fat oil and vinegar dressing (see *Shop Smart*, opposite)
Black peppercorns
Salt

SUNDAY NIGHT

CRISPY CHICKEN WITH RATATOUILLE (SAUTÉED PROVENÇAL VEGETABLES)

SERVES: 4
SERVING SIZE: 5 ounces chicken, 4 1/2 cups vegetables, 1 slice multigrain bread
PREP TIME: 15 minutes
COOKING TIME: 25 minutes

Freshly made ratatouille, a tasty blend of Provençal vegetables and crispy, sautéed chicken, makes a quick, colorful dinner. Coating the chicken with coarse cornmeal gives it a flavorful crust without having to deep-fry it. Cornmeal can be found in three textures, coarse, medium, or fine, and three colors, white, yellow, or blue, depending on the type of corn used.

HELPFUL HINTS:

- Any type of cornmeal can be used.
- Slice the eggplant and zucchini in a food processor fitted with a slicing blade and then cut into 1- to 2-inch pieces.
- Chicken in this recipe is for two meals. Half is stored for Tuesday's dinner.

COUNTDOWN:

- Start ratatouille.
- Make chicken

CRISPY CHICKEN

1/2 cup coarse cornmeal
1 teaspoon ground sage
1/4 teaspoon cayenne pepper
1/2 teaspoon salt
1/4 teaspoon freshly ground black pepper
2 egg whites
3 pounds boneless, skinless chicken thighs
3 tablespoons olive oil

1. Season cornmeal with ground sage, cayenne pepper, salt, and pepper and set aside in a shallow dish.

2. Lightly beat the egg whites. Remove visible fat from the chicken thighs and open them flat. Dip chicken into egg whites and then the cornmeal mixture, making sure both sides are well coated.

3. Heat olive oil in a large nonstick skillet over medium-high heat.

4. Add chicken and sauté 5 minutes. Turn and sauté 4 minutes. A meat thermometer inserted into chicken should read 175°F.

5. Place half the chicken (1 1/2 pounds) in a storage container and refrigerate for Tuesday's dinner. Serve the remaining chicken with the Ratatouille.

RATATOUILLE (SAUTÉED PROVENÇAL VEGETABLES)

1 pound eggplant, washed, unpeeled, and cut into 1- to 2-inch cubes (about 6 cups)
1 pound zucchini, washed and cut into 1- to 2-inch cubes (about 4 cups)
1/2 pound sliced button mushrooms (about 3 cups)
2 cups sliced onion
4 medium cloves garlic, crushed
3 cups low-sodium, no-sugar-added canned tomato sauce*
1/4 cup fresh oregano leaves OR 3 teaspoons dried oregano
4 teaspoons olive oil
1/4 teaspoon salt
1/4 teaspoon freshly ground black pepper
4 slices whole-meal, multigrain country bread

1. Add eggplant, zucchini, mushrooms, onion, garlic, and tomato sauce to a large saucepan. Stir to coat vegetables with the sauce. Place over medium-high heat for about 1–2 minutes or until the sauce starts to bubble slightly.

2. Lower heat to medium and cover. Simmer 15 minutes. Vegetables should be cooked through but a little firm.

3. Add oregano, olive oil, salt, and pepper. Serve bread with meal.

**Look for low-sodium tomato sauce containing per cup (8 ounces): 103 calories, 0.5 g fat, 21.3 g carbohydrate, 21 mg sodium.*

COST OF MEAL PER PERSON:

$4.28

PER SERVING

CHOICES/EXCHANGES
1 starch, 7 nonstarchy vegetable, 4 lean protein, 2 1/2 fat

Total Calories 550
Total Fat 19 g
Saturated Fat 3.8 g
Monounsaturated Fat 7.2 g
Trans Fat 0.0 g
Cholesterol 140 mg
Sodium 590 mg
Potassium 2010 mg
Total Carbohydrate 51 g
Fiber 12 g
Sugars 20 g
Protein 47 g
Phosphorus 530 mg

MONDAY NIGHT

SPAGHETTI AND MEATBALLS

SERVES: 4

SERVING SIZE: 5 ounces meatballs, 3/4 cup tomato sauce, 3/4 cup whole-wheat pasta, 2 cups salad

PREP TIME: 15 minutes

COOKING TIME: 20 minutes

Tasty, light meatballs in a rich pasta sauce are an American favorite. The meatballs in this recipe are made with lower-fat ground buffalo instead of ground beef. The addition of bread makes the meatballs light and fluffy. This meal uses half the ground buffalo. The remainder is used for Wednesday night's dinner.

HELPFUL HINTS:

- Any type of salad greens can be used for the salad.
- A food processor can be used to combine the ingredients. Try not to overprocess them. The meat will become too compact.
- A quick way to chop sage is to snip the leaves with a scissors.
- Use a flat spatula to turn the meatballs. A spoon might break the meatballs.

COUNTDOWN:

- Place a large pot of water for pasta on to boil.
- Make the meatballs.
- Cook the spaghetti.
- Make the salad.
- Complete the main dish.

SPAGHETTI AND MEATBALLS

1 slice whole-meal, multigrain bread
1 1/2 pounds lean ground buffalo
4 cloves garlic, crushed
2 teaspoons dried sage
1 cup chopped onion
2 large eggs
1/2 teaspoon salt
1/4 teaspoon freshly ground black pepper
1 tablespoon olive oil
1 1/2 cups low-sodium pasta sauce
1 1/2 cups water
1/2 pound whole-wheat spaghetti

1. Soak the bread in 1 cup water until soft.

2. Combine ground buffalo, garlic, sage, onion, and egg in a bowl or food processor. Remove bread from water and squeeze out excess water. Blend into meat mixture. Add salt and pepper. Form into balls about 2 1/2 inches in diameter. It should make 8 meatballs.

3. Heat olive oil in a medium-size nonstick skillet over medium-high heat. Brown the meatballs on all sides, about 5 minutes.

4. Mix the pasta sauce and water together. Lower the heat to medium and add the sauce and water mixture. Simmer gently 15 minutes, carefully turning the meatballs once. A meat thermometer inserted into meatballs should read 160°F.

5. While meatballs simmer, add the spaghetti to boiling water and cook 9 minutes or according to package instructions. Drain and divide spaghetti among 4 dinner plates. Serve meatballs and sauce over the spaghetti.

SALAD

8 cups shredded iceberg lettuce
4 tablespoons reduced-fat oil and vinegar dressing

1. Place lettuce in a salad bowl and toss with the dressing. Divide among 4 plates.

COST OF MEAL PER PERSON

$6.22

PER SERVING

CHOICES/EXCHANGES
3 1/2 starch, 1 nonstarchy vegetable, 6 lean protein

Total Calories 560
Total Fat 13 g
Saturated Fat 3.1 g
Monounsaturated Fat 4.7 g
Trans Fat 0.0 g
Cholesterol 205 mg
Sodium 480 mg
Potassium 1490 mg
Total Carbohydrate 60 g
Fiber 10 g
Sugars 10 g
Protein 51 g
Phosphorus 655 mg

TUESDAY NIGHT

CRISPY CHICKEN SANDWICH WITH SPICY COLESLAW

SERVES: 4

SERVING SIZE: 5 ounces chicken, 1 (3-ounce) whole-wheat roll, 1 cup coleslaw

PREP TIME: 15 minutes

COOKING TIME: 5 minutes

Use the second half of Sunday night's crispy chicken for this tasty sandwich. Sliced bread-and-butter pickles and spicy coleslaw are tasty accompaniments to this quick dinner.

It takes only minutes to make this coleslaw using shredded cabbage from the produce department.

HELPFUL HINTS:

- Any type of whole-wheat bread can be used.

COUNTDOWN:

- Make coleslaw.
- Toast rolls.
- Assemble sandwich.

CRISPY CHICKEN SANDWICH WITH SPICY COLESLAW

2 tablespoons reduced-fat mayonnaise
2 tablespoons distilled white vinegar
1/2 tablespoon Dijon mustard
2 teaspoons brown sugar
1/4 teaspoon freshly ground black pepper
4 cups washed, ready-to-eat shredded cabbage
4 whole-wheat kaiser rolls (3 ounces each)
Olive oil spray
1 1/2 pounds crispy chicken from Sunday night (page 8)
1/4 cup sliced bread-and-butter pickles

1. Mix mayonnaise, vinegar, mustard, and brown sugar together in a medium-size bowl. Add pepper. Add cabbage and toss well.

2. Open rolls and spray cut side with olive oil spray. Toast the rolls, cut side up, in a toaster oven or under a broiler until golden.

3. Place pickle slices on bottom half of the rolls. Place crispy chicken on top. Spoon coleslaw over the chicken and close the roll.

COST OF MEAL PER PERSON:
$2.53

PER SERVING

CHOICES/EXCHANGES
3 starch, 1/2 carbohydrate, 1 nonstarchy vegetable, 5 lean protein, 2 fat

Total Calories 600
Total Fat 21 g
Saturated Fat 3.8 g
Monounsaturated Fat 7.3 g
Trans Fat 0.0 g
Cholesterol 140 mg
Sodium 710 mg
Potassium 780 mg
Total Carbohydrate 57 g
Fiber 8 g
Sugars 14 g
Protein 43 g
Phosphorus 505 mg

WEDNESDAY NIGHT

SOUTHWESTERN BUFFALO SLIDERS WITH TACO SALAD

SERVES: 4

SERVING SIZE: 5 ounces buffalo burger (2 patties), 1 cup vegetables, 2 whole-wheat rolls (2 1/2 ounces total), 2 1/2 cups salad, 1 tablespoon dressing, 3/4 cup baked tortilla chips

PREP TIME: 15 minutes

COOKING TIME: 15 minutes

Enjoy earthy Southwestern flavors with these spicy buffalo sliders and taco salad.

Ground chipotle powder adds a spicy and smoky flavor to the burgers. The powder can also spice up many other foods—salad dressings, vegetables, potatoes, rice, and other meats.

HELPFUL HINTS:

- These burgers have a hot kick. If you're sensitive to hot spices, reduce the chipotle powder to 1 teaspoon, divided.

COUNTDOWN:

- Start burgers.
- While burgers cook, assemble salad.

SOUTHWESTERN BUFFALO SLIDERS

1 1/2 pounds ground buffalo
1/2 tablespoon chipotle powder, plus 1/2 teaspoon, divided
1/4 teaspoon salt
2 cups thinly sliced onion
2 cups thinly sliced red bell pepper
1/2 cup reduced-fat mayonnaise
8 whole-wheat slider rolls (mini hamburger rolls; 1 1/4 ounces each)

1. Mix ground buffalo with 1/2 tablespoon chipotle powder and salt. Form into 8 patties (about 3 inches in diameter).

2. Heat a large nonstick skillet over medium-high heat. Add the burgers, onion, and red pepper. Sauté 4 minutes. Turn burgers over and stir the vegetables. Sauté 4 more minutes. A meat thermometer inserted into burgers should read 160°F.

3. Cut slider rolls in half and open. Remove burgers from the skillet and place burgers on the bottom half of the 8 slider rolls.

4. Continue to cook the onion and red pepper for 2 to 3 minutes.

5. Mix the mayonnaise with the remaining 1/2 teaspoon chipotle powder and spread over the cut side of the tops of the rolls.

6. Spoon the onion and red peppers over the burgers and close with the roll tops.

TACO SALAD

8 cups shredded, washed, ready-to-eat iceberg lettuce
2 tomatoes, cut into cubes (about 2 cups)
4 tablespoons reduced-fat oil and vinegar dressing
3 cups low-fat baked tortilla chips (3 ounces)

1. Toss lettuce and tomato in a bowl with the dressing.

2. Break tortilla chips into bite-size pieces and sprinkle over the salad.

COST OF MEAL PER PERSON

$6.88

PER SERVING

CHOICES/EXCHANGES
3 starch, 2 nonstarchy vegetable, 5 lean protein, 1 1/2 fat

Total Calories 570
Total Fat 17 g
Saturated Fat 3.4 g
Monounsaturated Fat 4.5 g
Trans Fat 0.0 g
Cholesterol 110 mg
Sodium 710 mg
Potassium 1490 mg
Total Carbohydrate 54 g
Fiber 11 g
Sugars 13 g
Protein 46 g
Phosphorus 595 mg

THURSDAY NIGHT

BAKED PARMESAN SCALLOPS WITH SPINACH LINGUINE AND CARROTS

SERVES: 4
SERVING SIZE: 5 ounces scallops, 2 tablespoons bread crumb and cheese coating, 1 tablespoon wine sauce, 3/4 cup pasta, 1/2 cup vegetables, 2 tablespoons parsley
PREP TIME: 10 minutes
COOKING TIME: 20 minutes

Baked scallops are luscious served with linguine. Scallops are readily available. I like to use the frozen ones in this recipe so you can buy them on Sunday and use them on Thursday and Saturday. You can use any type of scallop for this recipe. If you buy small bay scallops, then cut the baking time to 10 minutes. This recipe uses half the scallops. The other half of the scallops are used for Saturday's dinner.

Fresh spinach linguine is available in the refrigerated case of most supermarkets. It only takes a couple of minutes to cook. Dried linguine also can be used. If you use dried, you will only need 6 ounces.

HELPFUL HINTS:

- Choose scallops that are wild caught and flash frozen.
- Fat-free, no-salt-added chicken broth can be used instead of clam juice.

COUNTDOWN:

- Preheat oven to 350°F.
- Place water for pasta on to boil.
- Start scallops.
- Make linguine.
- Complete scallops.

BAKED PARMESAN SCALLOPS

1 1/2 pounds frozen sea scallops, defrosted
1/2 cup whole-wheat plain bread crumbs
3 teaspoons butter
1/4 cup white wine
4 tablespoons freshly grated Parmesan cheese
1/4 teaspoon freshly ground black pepper
1/2 cup chopped fresh parsley

1. Preheat oven to 350°F.

2. Rinse scallops and place in a small baking dish just large enough to hold them in one layer. Sprinkle with bread crumbs and toss to coat. Cut butter into small pieces and spread over the scallops. Add wine to baking dish and bake for 15 minutes.

3. Remove scallops from oven and turn on broiler. Sprinkle scallops with Parmesan cheese and place under broiler for 5–10 seconds. Watch carefully—they will brown quickly. Remove from broiler and season with pepper. Serve on bed of Spinach Linguine and Carrots and sprinkle parsley on top.

SPINACH LINGUINE AND CARROTS

1 cup white wine, divided
1 cup sliced carrots
1 cup sliced onion
8 ounces fresh spinach linguine or 6 ounces dried linguine
1/4 teaspoon salt
1/4 teaspoon freshly ground black pepper

1. Place water for pasta on to boil.

2. Heat 1/2 cup wine in a small nonstick skillet. Add carrots and onion and sauté over low heat 10 minutes.

3. Place pasta in boiling water. Cook 2–3 minutes for fresh pasta and 9 minutes for dried. Save 4 tablespoons pasta water and then drain the linguine.

4. Add the reserved pasta water and remaining wine to the carrots and onions. Add salt and pepper. Add linguine to the sauce and toss well. Serve on individual plates and spoon scallops on top.

COST OF MEAL PER PERSON
$7.47

PER SERVING

CHOICES/EXCHANGES
3 starch, 1/2 carbohydrate, 1 nonstarchy vegetable, 5 lean protein

Total Calories 498
Total Fat 8.9g
Saturated Fat 3.8 g
Monounsaturated Fat 1.9 g
Sodium 701 mg
Cholesterol 112 mg
Total Carbohydrate 49.6 g
Fiber 4.5 g
Sugars 3.9 g
Protein 39.6 g
Potassium 382 mg
Phosphorus 220 mg

FRIDAY NIGHT

ORZO AND THREE-CHEESE "RISOTTO" WITH TOMATO AND ONION SALAD

SERVES: 4

SERVING SIZE: 3/4 cup pasta, 1/2 cup cheese sauce, 1 1/2 cups salad, 1 tablespoons dressing

PREP TIME: 10 minutes

COOKING TIME: 15 minutes

I created this recipe thinking it would make a quick substitute for baked macaroni. It turned out so creamy and delicious that it reminds me of an Italian risotto, but it's much easier to make.

HELPFUL HINTS:

- Crumbled feta cheese can be found in the dairy section of the supermarket.
- Turmeric or bijol may be substituted for saffron in the orzo dish.
- Onion is used in both recipes. To save time, dice all the onion at one time and use as needed.

COUNTDOWN:

- Make orzo.
- While orzo cooks, make the salad.

ORZO AND THREE-CHEESE "RISOTTO"

4 cups fat-free, no-salt-added chicken broth
1 teaspoon saffron strands
4 teaspoons olive oil
1 cup diced red onion
2/3 cup crumbled feta cheese (4 ounces)
2 cups uncooked orzo
1/2 cup nonfat ricotta cheese
1/4 cup skim milk
1/2 cup freshly grated Parmesan cheese
1/4 teaspoon cayenne pepper
1/4 teaspoon salt
1/4 teaspoon freshly ground black pepper

1. Bring broth, saffron, and oil to a boil in a large nonstick saucepan. Add onion, feta cheese, and orzo. Return to a boil and cook 8–9 minutes, stirring occasionally.

2. In a medium-size bowl, mix ricotta cheese, milk, Parmesan cheese, and cayenne pepper together.

3. Test orzo to make sure it is cooked thoroughly and cook another 1–2 minutes if necessary.

4. Stir in the ricotta mixture and add more cayenne if needed. Add salt and pepper. (If risotto seems dry, add 2–3 tablespoons warm water.)

TOMATO AND ONION SALAD

6 cups washed, ready-to-eat romaine lettuce, cut into bite-size pieces
2 ripe medium tomatoes, washed and cut into eighths
4 tablespoons reduced-fat oil and vinegar dressing
1/2 teaspoon salt
1/4 teaspoon freshly ground black pepper
1/4 cup diced red onion

1. Add lettuce and tomato to bowl and toss with dressing. Sprinkle salt, pepper, and diced onion on top.

COST OF MEAL PER PERSON
$2.75

PER SERVING

CHOICES/EXCHANGES
2 1/2 starch, 1/2 carbohydrate, 2 nonstarchy vegetable, 1 medium-fat protein, 1 fat

Total Calories 430
Total Fat 11 g
Saturated Fat 4.8
Monounsaturated Fat 3.8 g
Trans Fat 0.0 g
Cholesterol 25 mg
Sodium 660 mg
Potassium 980 mg
Total Carbohydrate 59 g
Fiber 5 g
Sugars 10 g
Protein 21 g
Phosphorus 455 mg

SATURDAY NIGHT

THAI PEANUT AND COCONUT SCALLOPS WITH GINGER RICE

SERVES: 4

SERVING SIZE: 5 ounces scallops, 1/4 cup peanut/coconut sauce, 2 cups spinach, 3/4 cup rice

PREP TIME: 10 minutes

COOKING TIME: 10 minutes

Scallops are perfect for a quick meal. They need no preparation and only take a few minutes to cook. For this recipe they are simmered in a flavorful sauce made from a mixture of peanut sauce and coconut milk. Both items can be found in the Asian section of the supermarket.

Basmati rice has a nutty flavor and smells a little like popcorn when cooking. The best kind of basmati rice is imported and can be found in some supermarkets. Texmati rice, grown in the U.S., is more readily available. Either one will work in this recipe.

HELPFUL HINTS:

- If microwaveable brown basmati rice is not available, use microwaveable brown rice instead.
- Whole-leaf frozen spinach may be used. Defrost and drain before using.
- Choose scallops that are wild caught and flash frozen.

COUNTDOWN:

- Start rice.
- Make scallops.
- Finish rice.

THAI PEANUT AND COCONUT SCALLOPS

4 tablespoons bottled peanut sauce
3/4 cup light coconut milk
1 1/2 pounds frozen sea scallops, defrosted
4 teaspoons canola oil
1/4 teaspoon freshly ground black pepper
8 cups washed, ready-to-eat spinach

1. Mix peanut sauce and coconut milk together. Set aside.

2. Rinse scallops. Heat canola oil in a large nonstick skillet over high heat. Add scallops, sauté 3 minutes, sprinkle with pepper, and remove to a plate.

3. Add sauce mixture and spinach to skillet and boil 2 minutes. Remove from heat and return scallops to skillet to warm in sauce. Serve over rice.

GINGER RICE

Microwaveable brown basmati rice (to make 3 cups cooked rice)
3 teaspoons ground ginger
1/4 teaspoon freshly ground black pepper

1. Microwave rice according to package instructions. Place 3 cups cooked rice in a bowl and mix in ginger and pepper.

COST OF MEAL
PER PERSON
$7.80

PER SERVING

CHOICES/EXCHANGES
2 1/2 starch, 1/2 carbohydrate, 1 nonstarchy vegetable, 4 lean protein, 1/2 fat

Total Calories 450
Total Fat 11 g
Saturated Fat 3.4 g
Monounsaturated Fat 3.5 g
Trans Fat 0.0 g
Cholesterol 55 mg
Sodium 650 mg
Potassium 485 mg
Total Carbohydrate 50 g
Fiber 5 g
Sugars 3 g
Protein 37 g
Phosphorus 190 mg

WEEK TWO

WEEKLY BUDGET
Average cost of a meal per person for the week is
$3.93

SUNDAY NIGHT

MUSSELS IN GARLIC TOMATO BROTH

Gather the family around the table and dig into a big bowl of steaming, tasty mussels. It's an easy, inexpensive, and delicious meal!

MONDAY NIGHT

HERB-CRUSTED PORK TENDERLOIN WITH LINGUINE AND GREEN BEANS

Fresh rosemary coats this pork tenderloin. Roast the pork on Monday and save half for a quick and easy barbecued pork sandwich dinner on Wednesday. Frozen green beans, picked at their peak and quickly frozen, keep much of their nutrient value. Buy them on Sunday and use them Monday and Saturday.

TUESDAY NIGHT

SICILIAN SWORDFISH WITH ROASTED BRUSSELS SPROUTS AND POTATOES

Enjoy the flavors of Sicily: tomatoes, olives, garlic, and raisins for a little sweet touch. Look for frozen swordfish steaks so you can buy them on Sunday and have them Tuesday.

WEDNESDAY NIGHT

BARBECUED PORK SANDWICH AND SALAD

This sweet, tangy barbecue sandwich will be a hit with your family. You can make this meal in just 10 minutes using roasted pork from Monday night!

THURSDAY NIGHT

FILIPINO CHICKEN ADOBO AND MICROWAVE RICE WITH RED BELL PEPPER

This sweet and sour dish is one of the national dishes of the Philippines. The chicken is cooked in a sauce of soy sauce, vinegar, and honey.

FRIDAY NIGHT

PESTO AND BEAN SOUP

The highlight of this vegetarian dinner is the pesto sauce. It gives body and flavor to this entrée-worthy soup.

SATURDAY NIGHT

CHICKEN CURRY WITH BROWN RICE

This simple curry dish is made with onion, garlic, apples, and green beans. It's finished with a flavor-packed apricot cream sauce.

SHOPPING LIST

SHOP SMART

- Look for barbecue sauce containing per tablespoon: 28 calories, 6.5 g carbohydrate, 199 mg sodium.
- Look for canned potatoes containing per cup: 112 calories, 0.36 g. fat, 24.5 g carbohydrate, 24 mg sodium.
- Look for reduced-fat oil and vinegar dressing containing per tablespoon: 11 calories, 1.0 g fat, 4 mg sodium.

Here is the Shopping List for this week's dinners.

This shopping list will help you get in and out of the market quickly. Ingredients are listed by supermarket department to make shopping easier; you won't forget something in one department and have to go back and forth across the store.

The amount needed of each ingredient is listed so you will know what size package or can to buy. If it helps you to better visualize the amount you need, please note that 4 tablespoons equal 1/4 cup and 8 tablespoons equal 1/2 cup.

Make sure to check your refrigerator and pantry to see if you have any of these ingredients on hand before making your trip to the market.

MEAT AND SEAFOOD
4 pounds fresh mussels
3 pounds pork tenderloin
1 1/2 pounds frozen swordfish steaks
3 pounds boneless, skinless chicken thighs

DAIRY
1 carton light cream (1/2 cup needed)

BAKERY
1 loaf whole-grain bread (4 slices needed)
4 whole-wheat kaiser rolls (2 ounces each)

CONDIMENTS

1 bottle barbecue sauce (6 tablespoons needed) (see *Shop Smart*, opposite)
1 bottle distilled vinegar (4 tablespoons needed)
1 small bottle reduced-sodium soy sauce (4 tablespoons needed)
1 small bottle honey (3 tablespoons needed)
1 small bottle hot pepper sauce
1 container fat-free, no-salt-added chicken broth (7 cups needed)
1 container reduced-fat pesto sauce (8 tablespoons needed)
1 jar apricot jam (3 tablespoons needed)

SPICE SECTION

1 small bottle dried oregano (2 teaspoons needed)
1 small bottle mild curry powder (2 tablespoons needed)

PASTA, RICE, DRIED FRUIT, NUTS

1/2 pound fresh whole-wheat linguine
1 small box raisins (4 tablespoons needed)
Microwaveable brown rice (to make 5 cups cooked rice)
1 package acini di pepe pasta, or other small pasta, such as orzo (2/3 cup needed)
1 small package pecan pieces (4 tablespoons needed)

CANNED/FROZEN VEGETABLES

2 pounds frozen green beans
1 can potatoes (2 pounds needed) (see *Shop Smart*, opposite)
1 can low-sodium diced tomatoes (2 cups needed)
1 container pitted black olives (10 needed)
1 package frozen diced onion (2 cups needed)
1 package frozen peas (1 cup needed)
1 can low-sodium cannellini beans (1 3/4 cups needed)

ALCOHOL AND WINE

1 small bottle dry white wine (1 cup needed)

PRODUCE

5 onions (6 cups needed)
1 bunch celery (2 cups sliced needed)
8 plum tomatoes
1 bunch fresh parsley (1/2 cup needed)
1 bunch fresh rosemary (3 tablespoons needed)
1 bunch fresh basil (1 cup needed)
1 package baby Brussels sprouts (4 cups needed)
1 bag washed, ready-to-eat salad greens (8 cups needed)
1 container cherry tomatoes (4 cups needed)
2 red bell peppers (2 cups needed)
1 bunch scallions (6 scallions needed)
2 Granny Smith apples (1 1/2 cups needed)

STAPLES

Balsamic vinegar
Flour
Garlic (23 cloves needed)
Olive oil
Olive oil spray
Reduced-fat oil and vinegar dressing (see *Shop Smart*, opposite)
Salt
Black peppercorns

SUNDAY NIGHT
MUSSELS IN GARLIC TOMATO BROTH

SERVES: 4
SERVING SIZE: 2 1/2 cups vegetables, 5 ounces mussels, 1 slice whole-grain bread, 1 cup broth
PREP TIME: 15 minutes
COOKING TIME: 10 minutes

Mussels steamed in a garlic, tomato, and white wine broth are easy and inexpensive to make. Store the mussels in the refrigerator. Wash the mussels in cold water before using, and scrape off the beard or thin hairs along the shell. The beard is how the mussel attaches itself to rocks. If any of the mussels are open, tap them gently, and discard any that do not close.

HELPFUL HINTS:

- Low-sodium fish broth can be substituted for the white wine, if preferred.
- Slice the vegetables in a food processor fitted with a thin slicing blade.

COUNTDOWN:

- Start vegetables.
- While vegetables cook, wash mussels.
- Finish dish.

MUSSELS IN GARLIC TOMATO BROTH

2 tablespoons olive oil
4 cups sliced onion
4 large cloves garlic, crushed
2 cups sliced celery
8 plum tomatoes, cut into large cubes (about 4 cups)
1 cup dry white wine
1/4 teaspoon freshly ground black pepper
4 pounds fresh mussels
1/2 cup chopped parsley
4 slices whole-grain bread

1. Heat the oil in a large saucepan over medium heat. Sauté the onion, garlic, celery, and tomatoes until they start to shrivel but not brown, about 5–6 minutes.

2. Add the white wine and freshly ground pepper and bring to a boil. Add the mussels and cover the saucepan tightly. Let boil about 3 minutes, shaking the pan several times. The wine will boil up over the mussels and they will open. As soon as they are open, take the pan off the heat. Do not overcook or the mussels will become rubbery.

3. To serve, lift the mussels out of the pan with a slotted spoon and place in 4 large soup bowls. Discard any mussels that do not open. Spoon broth over the mussels. Sprinkle with parsley and serve with slices of bread on the side. Spoon any remaining mussels that do not fit into the soup bowls into another bowl and serve them at the table for people to help themselves to more.

COST OF MEAL PER PERSON
$3.67

PER SERVING

CHOICES/EXCHANGES
1 starch, 5 nonstarchy vegetable, 2 lean protein, 1 1/2 fat

Total Calories 420
Total Fat 12 g
Saturated Fat 2.1 g
Monounsaturated Fat 4.4 g
Trans Fat 0.0 g
Cholesterol 50 mg
Sodium 610 mg
Potassium 1450 mg
Total Carbohydrate 41 g
Fiber 7 g
Sugars 13 g
Protein 26 g
Phosphorus 510 mg

MONDAY NIGHT

HERB-CRUSTED PORK TENDERLOIN WITH LINGUINE AND GREEN BEANS

SERVES: 4
SERVING SIZE: 5 ounces pork, 3/4 cup pasta, 1 cup vegetables
PREP TIME: 10 minutes
COOKING TIME: 30 minutes

Fresh rosemary and garlic coat this pork tenderloin as it roasts in the oven. Save time for Wednesday night's barbecued pork sandwich dinner by roasting all the pork tonight. Frozen green beans are used in the linguine dish. Frozen vegetables can be a good choice when they are picked at their peak and immediately frozen. Keep some on hand for other meals.

HELPFUL HINTS:

- Dried whole-wheat linguine can be used. Boil it for 5 minutes, add the green beans, and continue to boil for 3 minutes or until the linguine is cooked.

COUNTDOWN:

- Preheat oven to 400°F.
- Place water for pasta on to boil.
- Make pork.
- Make linguine.

HERB-CRUSTED PORK TENDERLOIN

3 pounds pork tenderloin
1 tablespoon olive oil
3 cloves garlic, crushed
3 tablespoons chopped fresh rosemary
1/4 teaspoon freshly ground black pepper

1. Preheat oven to 400°F. Line a large baking tray with foil.

2. Remove visible fat from the pork. Place the pork on the baking sheet and brush with olive oil. Press garlic, rosemary, and pepper into the pork on all sides.

3. Roast pork 25–30 minutes or until a meat thermometer inserted into pork reads 145°F.

4. Remove pork from oven and set half the pork aside for Wednesday's dinner (when pork is cool, wrap it and store in the refrigerator). Slice the remaining half of the pork and serve with the linguine and green beans.

LINGUINE AND GREEN BEANS

1/2 pound fresh whole-wheat linguine
1 pound trimmed frozen green beans, cut into 1-inch pieces
2 tablespoons olive oil
1/2 teaspoon salt

1. Bring a large saucepan filled with water to a boil. Add the linguine and green beans. Boil 3–4 minutes.

2. Remove 4 tablespoons of the cooking water to a bowl. Add the olive oil and salt to the bowl. Drain the linguine and green beans and add to the bowl. Toss well and serve.

COST OF MEAL PER PERSON

$3.22

PER SERVING

CHOICES/EXCHANGES
2 1/2 starch, 2 nonstarchy vegetable, 5 lean protein, 1 fat

Total Calories 510
Total Fat 13 g
Saturated Fat 2.7 g
Monounsaturated Fat 5.5 g
Trans Fat 0.0 g
Cholesterol 110 mg
Sodium 390 mg
Potassium 1060 mg
Total Carbohydrate 52 g
Fiber 6 g
Sugars 5 g
Protein 45 g
Phosphorus 575 mg

TUESDAY NIGHT

SICILIAN SWORDFISH WITH ROASTED BRUSSELS SPROUTS AND POTATOES

SERVES: 4
SERVING SIZE: 5 ounces swordfish, 1/2 cup sauce, 1 3/4 cups vegetables
PREP TIME: 15 minutes
COOKING TIME: 30 minutes

Tomatoes, olives, and garlic are staples of zesty Sicilian cooking. Raisins add sweetness, giving the sauce a tantalizing sweet and sour flavor. Make the sauce in a microwave oven and use frozen baby Brussels sprouts for a quick and easy dinner. Look for small baby Brussels sprouts in the freezer section.

HELPFUL HINTS:

- This sauce also goes well with chicken or beef.
- If frozen baby Brussels sprouts are not available, use large ones and cut them in quarters.
- Make sure your oven is at temperature before adding the Brussels sprouts.

COUNTDOWN:

- Preheat oven to 400°F.
- Prepare all ingredients.
- When oven is at temperature roast Brussels sprouts and potatoes.
- Make sauce.
- Sauté swordfish.

SICILIAN SWORDFISH

2 cups drained, canned, low-sodium diced tomatoes
6 cloves garlic, crushed
10 pitted black olives
4 tablespoons raisins
2 teaspoons dried oregano
1/4 teaspoon salt
1/4 teaspoon freshly ground black pepper
2 teaspoons olive oil
1 1/2 pounds frozen swordfish steaks, defrosted

1. To make sauce: Place tomatoes, garlic, olives, raisins, and oregano in a microwave-safe bowl. Cover with a paper towel and microwave on high 4 minutes. Add salt and pepper. Or place tomatoes and garlic in small saucepan and simmer 2 minutes. Add olives, raisins, and oregano and continue to cook 5 minutes. Add salt and pepper.

2. Heat oil in a large nonstick skillet over medium-high heat. Add the swordfish, making sure all steaks fit in one layer (use two skillets if needed). Sauté 2 minutes.

3. Turn and sauté 2 minutes for 1/2-inch steaks. (Cook 2 minutes longer for 1-inch steaks.) Divide among 4 plates and spoon sauce on top.

ROASTED BRUSSELS SPROUTS AND POTATOES

4 cups baby Brussels sprouts
2 pounds canned potatoes, rinsed and drained (about 3 cups)*
2 tablespoons olive oil
4 tablespoons balsamic vinegar
1/4 teaspoon salt
1/4 teaspoon freshly ground black pepper

1. Preheat oven to 400°F.

2. Remove stem end from Brussels sprouts and cut in half. Cut potatoes in half or into pieces about the same size as the Brussels sprouts. Line a baking sheet with foil. Add the oil and roll the potatoes and Brussels sprouts in the oil making sure all sides are covered. Sprinkle with salt and pepper and toss well.

3. Spread vegetables in one layer on the sheet. Roast 20 minutes. Remove from oven and turn potatoes and sprouts over. Roast another 10 minutes.

4. Remove vegetables to a bowl. Add the balsamic vinegar and toss well. Let rest while you make the fish.

**Canned potatoes containing per cup: 112 calories, 0.36 g fat, 24.5 g carbohydrate, 24 mg sodium*

COST OF MEAL PER PERSON

$6.25

PER SERVING

CHOICES/EXCHANGES
2 starch, 1/2 fruit,
3 nonstarchy vegetable,
4 lean protein, 2 fat

Total Calories 540
Total Fat 18 g
Saturated Fat 3.5 g
Monounsaturated Fat 7.9 g
Trans Fat 0.0 g
Cholesterol 65 mg
Sodium 580 mg
Potassium 735 mg
Total Carbohydrate 56 g
Fiber 12 g
Sugars 14 g
Protein 42 g
Phosphorus 100 mg

WEDNESDAY NIGHT

BARBECUED PORK SANDWICH AND SALAD

SERVES: 4
SERVING SIZE: 1 whole-wheat roll (2 ounces), 5 ounces pork, 1 1/2 tablespoons sauce, 3 cups salad, 2 tablespoons dressing
PREP TIME: 5 minutes
COOKING TIME: 5 minutes

This meal can be prepared in less than 10 minutes using the roast pork saved from Monday night.

HELPFUL HINTS:

- Any type of salad greens can be used.

COUNTDOWN:

- Assemble salad.
- Make pork sandwich.

BARBECUED PORK SANDWICH

4 whole-wheat kaiser rolls (2 ounces each)
1 1/2 pounds cooked pork tenderloin (saved from Monday night)
6 tablespoons barbecue sauce*

1. Open the rolls and toast. Set aside.

2. Cut pork into 1-inch slices and cut the slices into 1/2-inch strips.

3. Add barbecue sauce to a saucepan and add the pork. Place over medium heat. Stir 3–4 minutes to warm the pork and sauce. Divide the pork among the 4 rolls and serve with the salad.

**Barbecue sauce, containing per tablespoon: 28 calories, 6.5 g carbohydrate, 199 mg sodium.*

TOSSED SALAD

8 cups washed, ready-to-eat salad greens
4 cups cherry tomatoes
1/2 cup reduced-fat oil and vinegar dressing**

1. Place salad and tomatoes in a salad bowl and toss with the dressing.

*** Reduced-fat oil and vinegar dressing containing per tablespoon: 11 calories, 1.0 g fat, 4 mg sodium.*

COST OF MEAL PER PERSON

$4.50

PER SERVING

CHOICES/EXCHANGES
2 starch, 1/2 carbohydrate, 2 nonstarchy vegetable, 5 lean protein

Total Calories 460
Total Fat 9 g
Saturated Fat 2.2 g
Monounsaturated Fat 3.3 g
Trans Fat 0.0 g
Cholesterol 110 mg
Sodium 550 mg
Potassium 1605 mg
Total Carbohydrate 47 g
Fiber 9 g
Sugars 18 g
Protein 43 g
Phosphorus 640 mg

THURSDAY NIGHT

FILIPINO CHICKEN ADOBO AND MICROWAVE RICE WITH RED BELL PEPPER

SERVES: 4
SERVING SIZE: 5 ounces chicken, 1/2 cup sauce and vegetables, 3/4 cup rice, 3/4 cup vegetables
PREP TIME: 5 minutes
COOKING TIME: 25 minutes

Mild, tangy Chicken Adobo is one of the national dishes of the Philippines. The meat stews in a vinegar sauce as it is cooked slowly over low heat. This quick version of the dish has all of the flavors of classic chicken adobo without the hours of preparation. The chicken is cooked in the sauce, removed, and then sautéed for a few minutes.

HELPFUL HINTS:

- Sauté the chicken over a low flame so that it browns but does not burn.

COUNTDOWN:

- Start the chicken.
- While chicken cooks, make the rice.
- When ready, brown the chicken.

FILIPINO CHICKEN ADOBO

1 1/2 pounds boneless, skinless chicken thighs
1 cup sliced onion
4 tablespoons white distilled vinegar
4 tablespoons reduced-sodium soy sauce
3 tablespoons honey
6 cloves garlic, crushed
4 teaspoons olive oil

1. Remove visible fat from chicken. Add chicken, onion, vinegar, soy sauce, honey, and garlic to a large saucepan. Bring to a simmer over medium heat (do not boil) and cook, covered, 10 minutes.

2. Turn chicken over, lower heat to medium low, and cook, covered, another 5 minutes.

3. Remove chicken from the saucepan. A meat thermometer inserted into chicken should read 170°F.

4. Raise heat to high and reduce the sauce for about 4–5 minutes. Remove to a bowl.

5. To finish, pat chicken dry with a paper towel. Heat olive oil over medium-low heat in the saucepan and add chicken. Brown on one side 1 minute, then brown on second side 1 minute, stirring brown bits in the bottom of the pan. Divide among 4 dinner plates and serve sauce on top. Serve with rice.

MICROWAVE RICE WITH RED BELL PEPPER

Microwaveable brown rice (to make 3 cups cooked rice)
2 cups diced red bell pepper
4 scallions, sliced
4 teaspoons olive oil

1. Cook rice according to package instructions.

2. Measure 3 cups of rice and reserve any remaining rice for another dinner. Add the red bell pepper, scallions, and olive oil and toss well.

COST OF MEAL PER PERSON

$3.22

PER SERVING

CHOICES/EXCHANGES
2 starch, 1 1/2 carbohydrate, 2 nonstarchy vegetable, 5 lean protein, 1 fat

Total Calories 570
Total Fat 18 g
Saturated Fat 3.6 g
Monounsaturated Fat 7.2 g
Trans Fat 0.0 g
Cholesterol 140 mg
Sodium 670 mg
Potassium 780 mg
Total Carbohydrate 61 g
Fiber 5 g
Sugars 17 g
Protein 41 g
Phosphorus 490 mg

FRIDAY NIGHT

PESTO AND BEAN SOUP

SERVES: 4
SERVING SIZE: 4 cups vegetable and broth mixture
PREP TIME: 5 minutes
COOKING TIME: 25 minutes

A simple pesto sauce adds body and flavor to this soup. Using prepared reduced-fat pesto sauce shortens the preparation time. Make this a vegetarian meal by using low-sodium vegetable broth.

This recipe calls for acini di pepe, which is a very small pasta that is perfect for soups. You can use orzo, a rice-shaped pasta, or any type of small pasta in this dish. You can also use any leftover pasta you have; break it up into small, equal-size pieces.

HELPFUL HINTS:

- Great Northern beans can be substituted for cannellini beans.

COUNTDOWN:

- Prepare ingredients.
- Make soup.

PESTO AND BEAN SOUP

Olive oil spray
2 cups frozen chopped onion
5 cups fat-free, no-salt-added chicken broth
2 cups water
2/3 cup acini di pepe pasta
1 3/4 cups rinsed and drained, canned, low-sodium cannellini beans
4 tablespoons chopped pecans
1 cup frozen peas
Several drops hot pepper sauce
8 tablespoons reduced-fat pesto sauce
1 cup fresh basil, torn into bite-size pieces

1. Heat a large saucepan over high heat and spray with olive oil spray. Add onion and sauté, stirring, 2 minutes.

2. Add chicken broth, water, pasta, and beans. Reduce heat to medium and simmer, uncovered, 15 minutes.

3. Meanwhile toast the pecans in a toaster oven or under the broiler for 1–2 minutes. Watch them carefully. They can burn easily.

4. Add peas and hot pepper sauce to the saucepan and simmer 5 minutes.

5. Remove soup from heat and stir in pesto sauce and basil. Serve in 4 soup bowls and sprinkle pecans on top.

COST OF MEAL
PER PERSON
$3.40

PER SERVING

CHOICES/EXCHANGES
3 1/2 starch, 1 nonstarchy vegetable, 2 lean protein, 2 fat

Total Calories 470
Total Fat 17g
Saturated Fat 2.3 g
Monounsaturated Fat 7.7 g
Trans Fat 0.0 g
Cholesterol 5 mg
Sodium 450 mg
Potassium 1020 mg
Total Carbohydrate 59 g
Fiber 10 g
Sugars 10 g
Protein 24 g
Phosphorus 425 mg

SATURDAY NIGHT

CHICKEN CURRY WITH BROWN RICE

SERVES: 4
SERVING SIZE: 5 ounces chicken, 1 3/4 cups vegetables, 2/3 cup sauce, 1/2 cup rice
PREP TIME: 15 minutes
COOKING TIME: 15 minutes

This is a simple curry using store-bought curry powder. Strictly speaking, prepared curry powder doesn't really exist in India. Good cooks prefer to make their own blend of spices using the freshest ingredients. The curry powder found in the supermarket should be used within 3–4 months. After that, it loses some of its flavor.

Frozen green beans are used in this dish. I like to keep them on hand for a quick dinner. They can be a good alternative to fresh green beans. Vegetables grown for freezing are picked at their peak and flash frozen, which allows them to keep much of their nutrient value.

HELPFUL HINTS:

- If you like your curry spicy, use hot curry powder instead of mild.
- To help speed up cooking the curry, prepare and arrange the ingredients in order of use in the recipe. That way, you can easily add them to the skillet.

COUNTDOWN:

- Prepare ingredients.
- Make chicken curry.
- While chicken cooks, microwave the brown rice.

CHICKEN CURRY

Olive oil spray
1 1/2 pounds boneless, skinless chicken thighs
1 cup sliced onion
4 cloves garlic, crushed
2 tablespoons mild curry powder
1 1/2 cups Granny Smith apple cubes (about 1/2-inch cubes)
2 tablespoons flour
2 cups fat-free, no-salt-added chicken broth
1 pound frozen, cut green beans (about 4 cups)
3 tablespoons apricot jam
1/2 cup light cream
1/4 teaspoon salt
1/4 teaspoon freshly ground black pepper
2 scallions, sliced

1. Remove visible fat from chicken.

2. Heat a large nonstick skillet over medium-high heat. Spray with olive oil. Add the chicken and brown 3 minutes. Turn chicken and brown 3 more minutes, or until a meat thermometer inserted into chicken reaches 170°F.

3. Remove chicken from skillet and add the onion, garlic, and curry powder. Sauté 1 minute. Add the apple and flour. Stir to coat the ingredients with the flour. Add the chicken broth and green beans. Cook until sauce thickens, about 5 minutes.

4. Add apricot jam and cream. Stir to combine and melt jam. Return the chicken to the skillet and warm through, about 2 minutes. Sprinkle with salt and pepper. Serve over rice and sprinkle scallions on top.

BROWN RICE

Microwaveable brown rice (to make 2 cups cooked rice)
2 teaspoons olive oil

1. Cook rice according to package instructions.

2. Measure 2 cups of rice and reserve any remaining rice for another meal. Add the olive oil to rice and toss well.

COST OF MEAL PER PERSON

$3.28

PER SERVING

CHOICES/EXCHANGES
1 starch, 2 1/2 carbohydrate, 2 nonstarchy vegetable, 5 lean protein, 1 1/2 fat

Total Calories 570
Total Fat 19 g
Saturated Fat 6.3 g
Monounsaturated Fat 7.0 g
Trans Fat 0.0 g
Cholesterol 160 mg
Sodium 40 mg
Potassium 1060 mg
Total Carbohydrate 60 g
Fiber 9 g
Sugars 18 g
Protein 44 g
Phosphorus 545 mg

WEEK **THREE**

WEEKLY BUDGET
Average cost of a meal per person for the week is
$6.76

SUNDAY NIGHT
COFFEE-RUBBED STEAK WITH SAUTÉED GARLIC POTATOES

Coffee, smoked paprika, and chili powder add an intriguing flavor to strip steak. The garlic potatoes in this dish are started in the microwave to speed cooking and then sautéed. Half of the steak is saved for a quick Tuesday night fajita dinner.

MONDAY NIGHT
HONEY GINGER GLAZED CHICKEN WITH BROWN RICE SALAD

Honey, spicy mustard, and ginger glaze the chicken cutlets in this dish, keeping them moist. Cucumber cubes and tomatoes add color and crunch to the rice salad on the side. Extra rice is made and saved for Wednesday night's dinner.

TUESDAY NIGHT
BEEF FAJITAS WITH CORN SALAD

These Southwestern fajitas can be made in minutes using the saved, cooked steak from Sunday night. Corn and sliced red peppers over lettuce make a quick, tasty salad.

WEDNESDAY NIGHT
CHICKEN FRIED RICE

Using cold, cooked rice makes a better fried rice. The cooked rice left over from Monday night is perfect for this fried rice dish.

THURSDAY NIGHT
SHRIMP SCAMPI WITH BASIL LINGUINE

Large, juicy shrimp are smothered in garlic and wine for this Italian-American classic. The scampi is served over linguine sprinkled with fresh basil.

FRIDAY NIGHT
BLACK BEAN BURRITO WITH JICAMA STICKS

Black beans, flavored with ground cumin and coriander, are mixed with Monterey Jack cheese and ricotta cheese in this Mexican-themed vegetarian dinner. Jicama adds a crisp and juicy side dish.

SATURDAY NIGHT
SHRIMP AND MUSHROOM PIZZA

Enjoy a pizza night! Shrimp, mushrooms, and green pepper fill the pizza that is topped with spicy arugula leaves.

SHOPPING LIST

Here is the Shopping List for this week's dinners.

This shopping list will help you get in and out of the market quickly. The ingredients are listed by supermarket department to make shopping easier; you won't forget something in one department and have to go back and forth across the store.

The amount needed of each ingredient is listed so you will know what size package or can to buy. If it helps you to better visualize the amount you need, please note that 4 tablespoons equal 1/4 cup and 8 tablespoons equal 1/2 cup.

Make sure to check your refrigerator and pantry to see if you have any of these ingredients on hand before making your trip to the market.

MEAT AND SEAFOOD

3 pounds grass-fed strip steak
3 pounds chicken cutlets
3 pounds frozen, shelled large shrimp (wild caught or local)

DAIRY

1 carton nonfat ricotta cheese (1 1/2 cups needed)
1 small package reduced-fat Monterey Jack cheese (1 cup needed)
1 package reduced-fat Emmental cheese (8 ounces needed)

BAKERY

1 package 8-inch whole-wheat tortillas (8 tortillas needed)
1 (12-inch) whole-wheat pizza base (10 ounces)

SHOP SMART

- Look for reduced-fat oil and vinegar dressing containing per tablespoon: 11 calories, 1.0 g fat, 4 mg sodium.

CONDIMENTS

1 small bottle ground espresso coffee (1 tablespoon needed)
1 small bottle honey (3 tablespoons needed)
1 small bottle Dijon mustard (2 tablespoons needed)
1 small bottle sliced roasted red peppers (1 cup needed)
1 small bottle reduced-sodium soy sauce (4 tablespoons needed)
1 small bottle hot pepper sauce
1 small bottle sesame oil (4 tablespoons needed)

SPICE SECTION

1 small bottle onion powder (1 tablespoon needed)
1 small bottle smoked paprika (1 tablespoon needed)
1 small bottle chili powder (1 teaspoon needed)
1 small bottle ground cumin (2 teaspoons needed)
1 small bottle ground coriander (2 tablespoons needed)
1 small bottle dried oregano (2 teaspoons needed)

SUGAR AND FLOUR

1 small package brown sugar (1/2 tablespoon needed)

PASTA, RICE, DRIED FRUIT, NUTS

Microwaveable brown rice (to make 6 cups cooked rice)
1/2 pound fresh whole-wheat linguine

CANNED/FROZEN VEGETABLES

1 small package frozen corn kernels (2 cups needed)
1 small package frozen peas (4 cups needed)
Canned, no-salt-added black beans (2 cups rinsed needed)

ALCOHOL AND WINE

1 small bottle (or split) of red vermouth (1 1/2 cups needed)

PRODUCE

4 red bell peppers (4 cups needed)
4 green bell peppers (4 cups needed)
2 pounds red potatoes
4 medium onions (4 cups needed)
1 red onion (3/4 cup needed)
12 tomatoes
1 package sliced button mushrooms (2 cups needed)
1 small piece fresh ginger (2 tablespoons needed) or 1 bottle ground ginger
2 small jicamas
5 lemons (6 tablespoons)
1 cucumber (2 cups needed)
1 bag washed, ready-to-eat salad greens (9 cups needed)
1 package baby arugula (2 cups needed)
1 bunch scallions (6 needed)
1 bunch basil (1 cup needed)

STAPLES

Canola oil
Olive oil
Olive oil spray
Garlic (18 cloves needed)
Skim milk
Reduced-fat oil and vinegar dressing (see *Shop Smart*, opposite)
Salt
Black peppercorns

SUNDAY NIGHT

COFFEE-RUBBED STEAK WITH SAUTÉED GARLIC POTATOES

SERVES: 4
SERVING SIZE: 5 ounces steak, 1 cup tomatoes, 1/2 cup vegetables, 1 cup potato
PREP TIME: 15 minutes
COOKING TIME: 25 minutes

Coffee adds an intriguing flavor, smoked paprika gives a hint of smokiness, and chili powder gives a little kick and to this sautéed steak. The garlic potatoes are first cooked in the microwave oven and then sautéed in the same skillet used to cook the steak, which will save you clean up time.

HELPFUL HINTS:

- Grass-fed steak is now available in most supermarkets and is lower in saturated fat.
- Be sure to keep the heat on medium to medium-low (depending on your burners) while cooking the steak to keep the spice crust from burning.
- If your steak is thicker than 3/4 inch, lower the heat and cook it a little longer.

COUNTDOWN:

- Prepare ingredients.
- Microwave potatoes and set aside.
- Make steak.
- Remove steak to rest before slicing.
- Sauté potatoes using same skillet as steak.

COFFEE-RUBBED STEAK

1 tablespoon ground espresso coffee
1 tablespoon onion powder
1 tablespoon smoked paprika
1 teaspoon chili powder
1/2 tablespoon brown sugar
3 pounds grass-fed strip steak (about 3/4 inch thick), fat removed (half of steak saved for Tuesday night)
2 tablespoons olive oil
4 medium tomatoes, sliced

1. Mix coffee, onion powder, paprika, chili powder, and brown sugar together. Spread on both sides of the steak, pressing the spice mixture into the steak.

2. Heat oil in a large nonstick skillet over medium heat. Add the steak and sauté 5 minutes, watching to make sure the spices do not burn. Turn the steak over and cook another 5 minutes. A meat thermometer inserted into the steak should read 125°F for rare and 145°F for medium rare.

3. Remove to a cutting board and pour pan juices over the steak. Let rest while finishing the potatoes. Slice steak and save half of the steak for Tuesday night's dinner (wrap and place it in the refrigerator). Serve the remaining steak with sliced tomatoes on the side.

SAUTÉED GARLIC POTATOES

2 pounds red potatoes, unpeeled, washed, and cut into 1/2-inch pieces
6 cloves garlic, crushed
2 cups sliced red bell pepper
2 tablespoons olive oil
3/4 teaspoon salt
1/4 teaspoon freshly ground black pepper

1. Place potatoes in a microwave-safe bowl and microwave on high 10 minutes.

2. Remove from microwave and add garlic and red bell pepper. Set aside.

3. When steak is removed from skillet, add olive oil to the same skillet. Turn heat to high. Add potatoes, garlic, and red bell pepper. Sauté 10 minutes, turning the potatoes to brown on all sides. Add salt and pepper. Serve potatoes with the steak.

COST OF MEAL PER PERSON
$9.62

PER SERVING

CHOICES/EXCHANGES
2 1/2 starch,
2 nonstarchy vegetable,
5 lean protein, 1 fat

Total Calories 510
Total Fat 16 g
Saturated Fat 3.4 g
Monounsaturated Fat 6.7 g
Trans Fat 0.0 g
Cholesterol 95 mg
Sodium 600 mg
Potassium 2200 mg
Total Carbohydrate 50 g
Fiber 8 g
Sugars 11 g
Protein 46 g
Phosphorus 570 mg

MONDAY NIGHT

HONEY GINGER GLAZED CHICKEN WITH BROWN RICE SALAD

SERVES: 4

SERVING SIZE: 5 ounces chicken, 2 tablespoons glaze, 3/4 cup rice, 1 1/4 cups vegetables, 1 tablespoon salad dressing

PREP TIME: 15 minutes

COOKING TIME: 10 minutes

Honey, ginger, and spicy mustard make a sweet and tangy glaze for chicken cutlets. The cutlets are about 1/2 inch thick and take about 2 minutes per side to sauté. Then the sauce glazes the chicken, keeping it moist. This dinner uses half the chicken. The remainder is used for Wednesday night's dinner.

HELPFUL HINTS:

- Boneless, skinless chicken breasts can be used instead of chicken cutlets. Cook the breasts about 5 minutes per side. A meat thermometer inserted into the chicken should read 165°F.
- A quick way to chop fresh ginger is to peel it, cut it into small pieces, and press through a garlic press. Or you can grate the peeled ginger right into the sauce.

COUNTDOWN:

- Prepare ingredients.
- Make chicken.
- While chicken rests with the sauce, make the rice.

HONEY GINGER GLAZED CHICKEN

3 tablespoons honey
2 tablespoons Dijon mustard
4 teaspoons canola oil, divided
2 tablespoons chopped fresh ginger OR 1 teaspoon ground ginger
1 1/2 pounds chicken cutlets
1/4 teaspoon salt
1/4 teaspoon freshly ground black pepper

1. Combine honey, Dijon mustard, 2 teaspoons canola oil, and ginger together in a small bowl. Set aside.

2. Remove visible fat from chicken. Heat the remaining 2 teaspoons canola oil in a large nonstick skillet over medium-high heat. Add the chicken and sauté 2 minutes. Turn chicken over and sauté 2 minutes. A meat thermometer inserted into chicken should read 165°F. Sprinkle with salt and pepper.

3. Remove skillet from the heat and pour the glaze over the chicken, Cover the skillet with a lid and let sit 2–3 minutes while preparing the side dish.

BROWN RICE SALAD

Microwaveable brown rice (to make 6 cups cooked rice)
2 cups peeled, cubed cucumber
(cut into 1/4–1/2-inch cubes)
3 cups tomato cubes (cut into 1/4–1/2-inch cubes)
4 tablespoons reduced-fat oil and vinegar dressing
1/4 teaspoon salt
1/4 teaspoon freshly ground black pepper

1. Microwave rice according to package instructions.

2. Measure 3 cups rice, add to a bowl, and reserve remaining 3 cups for Wednesday's dinner. Add cucumber, tomato, dressing, and salt and pepper. Toss well.

COST OF MEAL
PER PERSON
$5.06

PER SERVING

CHOICES/EXCHANGES
2 1/2 starch, 1 carbohydrate,
1 nonstarchy vegetable,
5 lean protein

Total Calories 530
Total Fat 11 g
Saturated Fat 1.8 g
Monounsaturated Fat 5.1 g
Trans Fat 0.0 g
Cholesterol 125 mg
Sodium 470 mg
Potassium 1150 mg
Total Carbohydrate 60 g
Fiber 5 g
Sugars 19 g
Protein 44 g
Phosphorus 575 mg

TUESDAY NIGHT

BEEF FAJITAS WITH CORN SALAD

SERVES: 4

SERVING SIZE: 5 ounces steak, 1 cup vegetables, 1 whole-wheat tortilla, 2 3/4 cups salad, 1 tablespoon salad dressing

PREP TIME: 10 minutes

COOKING TIME: 10 minutes

Enjoy the earthy flavors of the Southwest with this steak fajita. Use the reserved steak from Sunday night to fill the fajitas. Corn and roasted red peppers give color and flavor to the salad side dish.

HELPFUL HINTS:

- Roasted red peppers are available in jars or cans in the condiment section of the supermarket.

COUNTDOWN:

- Make fajitas.
- Make salad.

BEEF FAJITAS

2 teaspoons canola oil
2 cups sliced onion (about 1/2-inch slices)
2 cups sliced green bell pepper
1 1/2 pounds sliced steak (saved from Sunday night)
1/2 teaspoon salt
4 (8-inch) whole-wheat tortillas

1. Heat oil in a large nonstick skillet over medium-high heat. Add the onion and green bell pepper. Sauté 5 minutes.

2. Add the sliced steak and sauté 2–3 minutes to warm the steak. Sprinkle with salt.

3. To serve, wrap the tortillas in paper towels and microwave on high 1 minute. Place the warm tortillas on 4 plates and divide the steak, onions, and peppers among them. Wrap and serve.

CORN SALAD

2 cups frozen corn kernels
8 cups washed, ready-to-eat salad greens
1 cup drained, sliced roasted red peppers
4 tablespoons reduced-fat vinaigrette dressing

1. Defrost corn by microwaving for 1 minute or by placing in a colander and running hot water over it.

2. Place greens in a salad bowl and add the corn and roasted red peppers. Sprinkle dressing over the salad. Toss well.

COST OF MEAL PER PERSON
$9.18

PER SERVING

CHOICES/EXCHANGES
2 starch, 2 nonstarchy vegetable, 5 lean protein, 1 fat

Total Calories 460
Total Fat 13 g
Saturated Fat 3.1 g
Monounsaturated Fat 5.8 g
Trans Fat 0.0 g
Cholesterol 95 mg
Sodium 520 mg
Potassium 1280 mg
Total Carbohydrate 43 g
Fiber 8 g
Sugars 10 g
Protein 47 g
Phosphorus 550 mg

WEDNESDAY NIGHT
CHICKEN FRIED RICE

SERVES: 4
SERVING SIZE: 5 ounces chicken, 2 1/4 cups vegetables, 3/4 cup rice
PREP TIME: 5 minutes
COOKING TIME: 15 minutes

This dinner uses the leftover cooked rice from Monday night, so it's quick and easy! In fact, using cold rice actually makes better fried rice.

HELPFUL HINTS:

- Place the frozen peas in a colander and run hot water over them to quickly defrost.
- The ingredients need to have space in the wok or skillet so that the food will be crisp, not steamed. If you don't have a very large wok or skillet, divide the recipe in half and cook each half separately.

COUNTDOWN:

- Stir-fry the chicken and remove.
- Stir-fry the remaining ingredients.

CHICKEN FRIED RICE

1 1/2 pounds chicken cutlets
4 tablespoons sesame oil, divided
3 cups brown rice (saved from Monday night)
2 cups sliced onion
6 cloves garlic, crushed
2 cups sliced red bell peppers
4 cups frozen peas, defrosted
4 tablespoons reduced-sodium soy sauce
6 scallions, sliced

1. Cut chicken into 1/4-inch strips. Heat 1 tablespoon sesame oil in a large wok or skillet over high heat. When it is smoking, add the chicken and stir-fry for 2–3 minutes, tossing to make sure all sides are browned. Remove to a plate.

2. Add 2 tablespoons sesame oil to the wok or skillet along with the brown rice, onion, garlic, and red bell pepper. Stir-fry for 4–5 minutes.

3. Add the peas and toss to combine with the other ingredients. Draw ingredients to the side of the wok or skillet and add the soy sauce in the center. Bring the ingredients into the center and stir-fry to combine them with the soy sauce.

4. Return the chicken to the wok or skillet and toss well. Remove from the heat and add the remaining 1 tablespoon sesame oil. Divide rice among 4 plates and sprinkle scallions on top.

COST OF MEAL
PER PERSON
$5.58

PER SERVING

CHOICES/EXCHANGES
3 starch, 2 nonstarchy vegetable,
5 lean protein, 2 fat

Total Calories 600
Total Fat 20 g
Saturated Fat 3.4 g
Monounsaturated Fat 7.1 g
Trans Fat 0.0 g
Cholesterol 125 mg
Sodium 610 mg
Potassium 1155 mg
Total Carbohydrate 56 g
Fiber 8 g
Sugars 9 g
Protein 48 g
Phosphorus 620 mg

THURSDAY NIGHT

SHRIMP SCAMPI WITH BASIL LINGUINE

SERVES: 4
SERVING SIZE: 5 ounces shrimp, 1/3 cup sauce, 3/4 cup whole-wheat linguine, 1/4 cup basil
PREP TIME: 10 minutes
COOKING TIME: 10 minutes

Large shrimp smothered in garlic and wine is an Italian-American classic. To Italians, "scampi" is the term for a small lobster called a prawn. However, in America scampi became a term for the sauce that goes with this shrimp dish. For this quick scampi, I teamed red vermouth, garlic, and parsley with the tender shrimp. American wild shrimp are juicy and plump. I recommend using these if they are available.

Basil and olive oil tossed with linguine makes a quick, hearty side dish.

HELPFUL HINTS:

- Dried linguine can be used instead of fresh. If using dried linguine, boil for 8–9 minutes.
- The quickest way to chop parsley and basil is to snip the leaves with a scissors.

COUNTDOWN:

- Place water for linguine on to boil.
- Make shrimp.
- Cook linguine.

SHRIMP SCAMPI

4 teaspoons olive oil
6 cloves garlic, crushed
1 1/2 cups red vermouth
1 1/2 pounds frozen, shelled large shrimp, defrosted
Several drops hot pepper sauce
1/4 teaspoon salt
1/4 teaspoon freshly ground black pepper

1. Heat olive oil in a large nonstick skillet over medium-high heat and add garlic and vermouth. Cook 2 minutes.

2. Add shrimp and cook 2–3 minutes until shrimp are pink. Add hot pepper sauce and salt and pepper. Remove shrimp from skillet.

3. Raise the heat and reduce sauce by half. Serve the sauce over the shrimp.

BASIL LINGUINE

1/2 pound fresh whole-wheat linguine
4 teaspoons olive oil
1 cup fresh basil
1/4 teaspoon salt
1/4 teaspoon freshly ground black pepper

1. In a large saucepan, bring 3–4 quarts water to a boil. Add linguine and boil 2–3 minutes for fresh linguine or 8–9 minutes for dried linguine.

2. Remove 2 tablespoons cooking water to a bowl and reserve. Add olive oil to the bowl.

3. Drain linguine and add to bowl with reserved water and olive oil. Toss well. Add the basil and salt and pepper. Toss and serve.

COST OF MEAL PER PERSON

$6.72

PER SERVING

CHOICES/EXCHANGES
2 1/2 starch, 1 carbohydrate, 5 lean protein, 1/2 fat

Total Calories 520
Total Fat 12 g
Saturated Fat 1.7 g
Monounsaturated Fat 4.7 g
Trans Fat 0.0 g
Cholesterol 275 mg
Sodium 500 mg
Potassium 740 mg
Total Carbohydrate 51 g
Fiber 6 g
Sugars 6 g
Protein 43 g
Phosphorus 570 mg

FRIDAY NIGHT

BLACK BEAN BURRITO WITH JICAMA STICKS

SERVES: 4
SERVING SIZE: 1/2 cup black beans, 1/2 cup cheese/onion mixture, 1 whole-wheat tortilla, 3/4 cup jicama
PREP TIME: 15 minutes
COOKING TIME: 5 minutes

Black beans, vegetables, and whole-wheat tortillas come together in this simple vegetarian dinner. Jicama is a root with a thin tan-colored skin that looks like a turnip. When peeled, it's crisp and juicy. In Mexico it's eaten raw, seasoned with a little lemon juice. Once peeled, cut, or sliced, it retains its texture and color.

HELPFUL HINTS:

- Red kidney beans can be used instead of black beans.
- Shredded Mexican-style reduced-fat cheese can be used instead of reduced-fat Monterey Jack cheese.

COUNTDOWN:

- Prepare jicama sticks.
- Make burrito.

BLACK BEAN BURRITO

1 1/2 cups nonfat ricotta cheese
2 tablespoons skim milk
3/4 cup chopped red onion
2 teaspoons ground cumin
2 tablespoons ground coriander
2 cups rinsed and drained, canned, no-salt-added, black beans
1 cup shredded, reduced-fat Monterey Jack cheese, divided
4 (8-inch) whole-wheat tortillas
3 tomatoes, sliced

1. Mix ricotta cheese, skim milk, onion, ground cumin, and ground coriander together. Add the black beans and 1/2 cup Monterey Jack cheese. Mix well.

2. Wrap tortillas in a paper towel and warm in a microwave oven for 10 seconds or place them unwrapped in a toaster oven for 20 seconds. This will make them easier to roll.

3. Place the tortillas on a countertop and spread tortillas with the ricotta mixture. Roll up the tortillas and place on a microwave-safe plate. Sprinkle remaining 1/2 cup cheese over the tortillas. Microwave 1 minute on high or until cheese melts.

4. Cut in half crosswise and serve with sliced tomatoes on the side.

JICAMA STICKS

2 small jicamas (about 3 cups peeled and cut into sticks)
2 tablespoons lemon juice
Several lettuce leaves

1. Peel jicama. Cut into 4 (1/2-inch) slices. Cut the slices into 1/2-inch sticks.

2. Toss with lemon juice. Place lettuce on the 4 dinner plates. Add the jicama slices.

COST OF MEAL PER PERSON

$2.63

PER SERVING

CHOICES/EXCHANGES
3 starch, 1/2 carbohydrate, 2 nonstarchy vegetable, 2 lean protein, 1/2 fat

Total Calories 440
Total Fat 9 g
Saturated Fat 4.8 g
Monounsaturated Fat 1.9 g
Trans Fat 0.0 g
Cholesterol 20 mg
Sodium 540 mg
Potassium 1195 mg
Total Carbohydrate 60 g
Fiber 18 g
Sugars 11 g
Protein 28 g
Phosphorus 580 mg

SATURDAY NIGHT

SHRIMP AND MUSHROOM PIZZA

SERVES: 4
SERVING SIZE: 5 ounces shrimp, 2 cups vegetables, 2 ounces cheese, 2.5 ounces pizza base
PREP TIME: 10 minutes
COOKING TIME: 20 minutes

A hint of lemon makes all the difference in this quick, delicious pizza. Arugula tops the pizza; its peppery flavor adds another dimension to this dish. Thin-crust pizza bases are available in the supermarket. It makes a crisp base for the pizza.

The order you add the ingredients makes a difference in how fast the pizza cooks. I place the mushrooms, peppers, and shrimp on top so that they are exposed to the heat and will cook through in just 15 minutes.

HELPFUL HINTS:

- Any type of mushrooms can be used for this pizza.

COUNTDOWN:

- Preheat oven to 400°F.
- Prepare pizza.
- Bake pizza.

SHRIMP AND MUSHROOM PIZZA

1 (12-inch) whole-wheat pizza base (10 ounces)
Olive oil spray
2 large ripe tomatoes, sliced (about 2 cups)
8 ounces reduced-fat Swiss cheese
2 cups sliced button mushrooms
2 cups sliced green bell pepper
1 1/2 pounds raw, peeled and deveined large shrimp
2 teaspoons dried oregano
4 tablespoons lemon juice
1/4 teaspoon freshly ground black pepper
2 cups baby arugula

1. Preheat oven to 400°F. Line a baking sheet with foil. Place pizza base on foil and spray with olive oil spray.

2. Place sliced tomatoes in one layer over the pizza base. Place cheese slices over tomatoes. Spread mushrooms over the cheese and bell pepper on top of the mushrooms. Place the shrimp evenly over the top. Sprinkle oregano over the shrimp.

3. Place baking tray on the middle shelf of the oven and bake 15 minutes. Remove from the oven and sprinkle the lemon juice and pepper over the top. Wash and dry the arugula, place in the center of the pizza, and spray with olive oil spray. Serve immediately.

COST OF MEAL
PER PERSON
$8.50

PER SERVING

CHOICES/EXCHANGES
2 starch, 2 nonstarchy vegetable, 6 lean protein

Total Calories 470
Total Fat 9 g
Saturated Fat 3.7 g
Monounsaturated Fat 3.1 g
Trans Fat 0.0 g
Cholesterol 295 mg
Sodium 670 mg
Potassium 1030 mg
Total Carbohydrate 44 g
Fiber 9 g
Sugars 9 g
Protein 60 g
Phosphorus 770 mg

WEEK **FOUR**

WEEKLY BUDGET
Average cost of a meal per person for the week is
$4.82

SUNDAY NIGHT
PATTY MELT WITH PICKLE RELISH SALAD

Enjoy this juicy burger smothered with caramelized onions and topped with melted cheese. Sweet pickle relish added to the dressing flavors the salad.

MONDAY NIGHT
BRONZED TILAPIA WITH RICE AND SPINACH PILAF

Tilapia fillets have a golden, caramelized coating with this bronzing method. Rice flavored with tomato juice and spinach completes the meal. Extra tilapia is cooked and saved for Wednesday night's dinner.

TUESDAY NIGHT
POULET AUX TOMATES (CHICKEN WITH TOMATOES) WITH NOUILLES AVEC PARMESAN (EGG NOODLES WITH PARMESAN)

Picture sitting in a French bistro as you're eating this popular bistro meal. The chicken is cooked in an onion tomato sauce and the noodles are topped with freshly grated Parmesan cheese.

WEDNESDAY NIGHT
FISH CAKES WITH QUICK COLESLAW

Add some scallions, Worcestershire sauce, and mayonnaise to the extra tilapia from Monday night's dinner to make these delightful fish cakes. Freshly made coleslaw using ready-to-eat sliced cabbage from the supermarket makes a crunchy, bright side dish.

THURSDAY NIGHT
SLOPPY JOES WITH SALAD

Ground beef in tomato sauce served in an open sandwich is an American favorite. These Sloppy Joes are served with a romaine and tomato salad.

FRIDAY NIGHT
PASTA PRIMAVERA

Linguine, fresh vegetables, toasted walnuts, basil, and Parmesan cheese make a light vegetarian dinner. You can add any extra leftover vegetables from the week.

SATURDAY NIGHT
FIVE-SPICE CHICKEN WITH CHINESE NOODLES

Chinese five-spice powder adds an aromatic flavor to chicken for this Chinese dinner. Chinese noodles coated with sesame oil and topped with fresh scallions complete the dinner.

SHOPPING LIST

Here is the Shopping List for this week's dinners.

This shopping list will help you get in and out of the market quickly. The ingredients are listed by supermarket department to make shopping easier; you won't forget something in one department and have to go back and forth across the store.

The amount needed of each ingredient is listed so you will know what size package or can to buy. If it helps you to better visualize the amount you need, please note that 4 tablespoons equal 1/4 cup and 8 tablespoons equal 1/2 cup.

Make sure to check your refrigerator and pantry to see if you have any of these ingredients on hand before making your trip to the market.

MEAT AND SEAFOOD
3 pounds 95% lean ground beef
3 pounds tilapia fillets
3 pounds boneless, skinless chicken breasts

DAIRY
4 ounces sliced reduced-fat Swiss cheese
1 small carton light cream (1/4 cup needed)
1 small piece Parmesan cheese (3/4 cup grated needed)
1 carton eggs (4 needed)

BAKERY
Whole-wheat bread (8 slices needed)
1 small container whole-wheat bread crumbs (1 cup needed)
1 whole-wheat baguette (8 ounces needed)
4 whole-wheat kaiser rolls (2 ounces each)

SHOP SMART

- Look for low-sodium tomato sauce containing per cup (8 ounces): 103 calories, 0.5 g fat, 21.3 g carbohydrate, 21 mg sodium.
- Look for reduced-fat oil and vinegar dressing containing per tablespoon: 11 calories, 1.0 g fat, 4 mg sodium.

CONDIMENTS

1 bottle reduced-sodium Worcestershire sauce
(6 tablespoons needed)
1 small bottle sweet pickle relish (4 tablespoons needed)
1 small bottle hot pepper sauce
1 small bottle distilled white vinegar (8 tablespoons needed)
1 bottle Chinese rice vinegar (3/4 cup needed)
1 small bottle reduced-sodium soy sauce
(3 tablespoons needed)
1 small bottle sesame oil (15 teaspoons needed)
1 bottle reduced-fat mayonnaise (8 tablespoons needed)
1 package sugar substitute (such as natural stevia)

SPICE SECTION

1 small bottle cayenne pepper (3 teaspoons needed)
1 small bottle garlic powder (4 teaspoons needed)
1 small bottle dried oregano (8 teaspoons needed)
1 small bottle dried thyme (4 teaspoons needed)
1 bottle Chinese five-spice powder (8 teaspoons needed)

PASTA, RICE, DRIED FRUIT, NUTS

1 small package long-grain brown rice (1 cup needed)
1 small package broad spinach (or plain) egg noodles
(1/2 pound needed)
1 package whole-wheat linguine (1/2 pound needed)
1 small package walnuts (1 cup needed)
1 small package steamed or fresh Chinese noodles
(dried can be used also; 1/2 pound needed)

CANNED/FROZEN VEGETABLES

1 can low-sodium, no-sugar-added canned tomato sauce
(3 1/2 cups needed) (see *Shop Smart*, opposite)

ALCOHOL, WINE, JUICE

1 small bottle tomato juice (32 ounces needed)

PRODUCE

8 medium onions (8 cups needed)
2 red onions (1 3/4 cups needed)
4 red bell peppers (4 cups needed)
2 green bell peppers (2 cups needed)
1 cucumber (2 cups needed)
1 small package sliced button mushrooms (2 cups needed)
1 package washed, ready-to-eat salad greens
(8 cups needed)
1 package washed, ready-to-eat romaine lettuce
(8 cups needed)
1 package washed, ready-to-eat spinach (8 cups needed)
1 package ready-to-eat sliced coleslaw (4 cups needed)
10 medium tomatoes
3 plum tomatoes
1/2 pound broccoli (3 cups needed)
1 bunch parsley (4 tablespoons needed)
1 bunch basil (1 cup needed)
3 bunches scallions (18 scallions needed)

STAPLES

Canola oil
Olive oil
Olive oil spray
Garlic (4 cloves needed)
Minced garlic (10 teaspoons needed)
Reduced-fat oil and vinegar dressing
(see *Shop Smart*, opposite)
Salt
Black peppercorns

SUNDAY NIGHT

PATTY MELT WITH PICKLE RELISH SALAD

SERVES: 4
SERVING SIZE: 5 ounces beef, 1 cup onions, 1 slice cheese, 3 cups salad, 2 tablespoons dressing
PREP TIME: 15 minutes
COOKING TIME: 20 minutes

Enjoy this juicy Patty Melt! Originally the patty melt was created as a thin burger, smothered with caramelized onions, topped with melted cheese, and served on rye bread. This dinner uses half the ground beef. The remainder is saved for Thursday night's dinner.

It can take a while to caramelize onions. I speed it up by starting them in the microwave first and then they only need about 10 minutes in a skillet.

HELPFUL HINTS:

- Any type of sliced whole-grain bread can be used.

COUNTDOWN:

- Start onions in microwave.
- Prepare the remaining ingredients and make the hamburger patties.
- While the onions sauté, assemble the salad.
- Finish the patty melt.

PATTY MELT

4 cups sliced onion
4 teaspoons canola oil, divided
1 1/2 pounds 95% lean ground beef
2 tablespoons reduced-sodium Worcestershire sauce
1/4 teaspoon salt
1/4 teaspoon freshly ground black pepper
4 slices reduced-fat Swiss cheese (4 ounces)
8 slices whole-wheat bread

1. Place onions in a microwave-safe bowl and microwave on high 5 minutes.

2. Heat 2 teaspoons oil in a large nonstick skillet over medium-low heat. Add the onions and sauté 10 minutes. They should be a golden color.

3. Meanwhile mix the ground beef and Worcestershire sauce together and add salt and pepper. Form into 4 thin patties.

4. Remove onions to a plate. Add the remaining oil and the patties to the same skillet. Brown patties on one side for 2 minutes. Turn over and cover each patty with 1 slice of cheese. Cover the skillet with a lid and cook about 1 minute or until cheese melts. A meat thermometer inserted into patties should read 160°F.

5. Toast the bread. Place 4 slices of bread on 4 plates. Place a patty on each of the 4 slices. Cover the patties with onions. Close the sandwiches with the remaining 4 slices of bread.

PICKLE RELISH SALAD

4 tablespoons sweet pickle relish
4 tablespoons reduced-fat oil and vinegar dressing*
8 cups washed, ready-to-eat salad greens
2 cups sliced red bell pepper
2 cups peeled and sliced cucumber

1. Add relish and dressing to a large bowl. Mix well.

2. Add the salad greens, red bell pepper, and cucumber and toss with the dressing.

**Look for reduced-fat oil and vinegar dressing containing per tablespoon: 11 calories, 1.0 g fat, 4 mg sodium.*

COST OF MEAL
PER PERSON
$5.01

PER SERVING

CHOICES/EXCHANGES
2 starch, 1/2 carbohydrate,
3 nonstarchy vegetable,
6 lean protein, 1 1/2 fat

Total Calories 590
Total Fat 18 g
Saturated Fat 5.6 g
Monounsaturated Fat 7.4 g
Trans Fat 0.0 g
Cholesterol 120 mg
Sodium 660 mg
Potassium 1415 mg
Total Carbohydrate 51 g
Fiber 9 g
Sugars 19 g
Protein 52 g
Phosphorus 735 mg

MONDAY NIGHT

BRONZED TILAPIA WITH RICE AND SPINACH PILAF

SERVES: 4
SERVING SIZE: 5 ounces tilapia, 2 teaspoons coating, 3/4 cup rice, 2 cups spinach, 1 cup sauce
PREP TIME: 5 minutes
COOKING TIME: 45 minutes

This tilapia is golden and caramelized, or "bronzed," from the cooking method. The secret to bronzing is to keep the skillet at a medium temperature. The tilapia should take 4–5 minutes to cook. Bring the fish to room temperature before cooking; this creates more even cooking.

The Spinach Rice Pilaf recipe is easy to make and takes less than 20 minutes to cook. To make this recipe even quicker to prepare, you can use a quick-cooking rice and stir the spinach into the rice as soon as the rice is cooked. The spinach will wilt in the heat of the cooked rice.

HELPFUL HINTS:

- Use two skillets if your large skillet does not fit all the tilapia in one layer.

COUNTDOWN:

- Start rice.
- Make tilapia.
- Finish rice.

BRONZED TILAPIA

3 teaspoons cayenne pepper
4 teaspoons garlic powder
8 teaspoons dried oregano
4 teaspoons dried thyme
3 pounds tilapia fillets
2 tablespoons olive oil

1. Mix cayenne pepper, garlic powder, oregano, and thyme together in a small bowl.

2. Place the tilapia on a large plate or cutting board and spoon half of the spice mixture onto one side of the tilapia fillets.

3. Heat a large nonstick skillet over high heat and add oil. When it is very hot, add the tilapia, seasoned side down. Lower heat to medium. Spread remaining spice mixture on the top side of tilapia fillets. Cook until the underside is bronze in color, 2–3 minutes.

4. Turn and cook second side 2–3 minutes or until cooked through.

5. Remove half the fillets, and cover and refrigerate them for Wednesday's fish cakes. Serve the remaining fillets with pilaf.

RICE AND SPINACH PILAF

2 tablespoons olive oil
1 cup long-grain brown rice
4 cups tomato juice
8 cups washed, ready-to-eat spinach
1/4 teaspoon salt
1/4 teaspoon freshly ground black pepper

1. Heat olive oil in a large nonstick skillet over medium-high heat. Add rice and sauté 1 minute.

2. Add tomato juice, stir, and bring to a simmer over lower heat. Cover and gently simmer 45 minutes. If pan becomes dry, add a little water.

3. Stir in the spinach and toss until it wilts. Add salt and pepper and serve.

COST OF MEAL PER PERSON

$4.37

PER SERVING

CHOICES/EXCHANGES
2 1/2 starch, 2 nonstarchy vegetable, 5 lean protein, 1 1/2 fat

Total Calories 520
Total Fat 18 g
Saturated Fat 3.6 g
Monounsaturated Fat 8.1 g
Trans Fat 0.0 g
Cholesterol 85 mg
Sodium 310 mg
Potassium 590 mg
Total Carbohydrate 51 g
Fiber 5 g
Sugars 10 g
Protein 42 g
Phosphorus 195 mg

TUESDAY NIGHT

POULET AUX TOMATES (CHICKEN WITH TOMATOES) WITH NOUILLES AVEC PARMESAN (EGG NOODLES WITH PARMESAN)

SERVES: 4
SERVING SIZE: 5 ounces chicken, 1 1/2 cups vegetables, 1 tablespoon cream, 3/4 cup egg noodles, 1 tablespoon cheese
PREP TIME: 10 minutes
COOKING TIME: 20 minutes

Enjoy this popular French bistro dish with fresh tomatoes, onions, and a touch of cream. The secret to the dish is to cook the onions until they are golden and sweet. To speed their cooking, the onions are microwaved first, then sautéed.

HELPFUL HINTS:

- Plain egg noodles can be used.
- A quick way to chop parsley is to snip the leaves with a scissors.

COUNTDOWN:

- Place water for noodles on to boil.
- Make chicken dish.
- While chicken cooks, make noodles.

POULET AUX TOMATES (CHICKEN WITH TOMATOES)

2 cups sliced onion
2 teaspoons olive oil
1 1/2 pounds boneless, skinless chicken breasts
4 cups chopped tomatoes (cut into 1/2–1-inch pieces)
1/4 teaspoon salt
1/2 teaspoon freshly ground black pepper
1/4 cup light cream
4 tablespoons chopped parsley

1. Place onions in a microwave-safe bowl and microwave on high 4 minutes.

2. Heat oil in a large nonstick skillet over medium-high heat. Add the microwaved onions and sauté 5 minutes.

3. Add the chicken and brown 2 minutes, turn over, and brown 2 more minutes. Add the tomatoes, reduce heat to medium, cover with a lid, and let cook gently 5 minutes. A meat thermometer inserted into chicken should read 165°F. Add salt and pepper. Remove the chicken to 4 dinner plates.

4. Add cream to the tomato mixture in the skillet and stir to combine. Spoon sauce over chicken and sprinkle with chopped parsley.

NOUILLES AVEC PARMESAN (EGG NOODLES WITH PARMESAN)

1/2 pound broad spinach egg noodles
4 teaspoons olive oil
1/4 teaspoon salt
1/2 teaspoon freshly ground black pepper
4 tablespoons freshly grated Parmesan cheese

1. Fill a large saucepan 3/4 full with water and bring to a boil. Add noodles and stir. Bring water back to a boil and cook for 7 minutes or until noodles are cooked but firm.

2. Drain noodles and toss with olive oil and salt and pepper. Divide among 4 dinner plates and sprinkle Parmesan cheese on top.

COST OF MEAL PER PERSON

$4.87

PER SERVING

CHOICES/EXCHANGES
2 1/2 starch, 3 nonstarchy vegetable, 5 lean protein, 2 fat

Total Calories 590
Total Fat 19 g
Saturated Fat 5.3 g
Monounsaturated Fat 6.4 g
Trans Fat 0.0 g
Cholesterol 190 mg
Sodium 490 mg
Potassium 1275 mg
Total Carbohydrate 55 g
Fiber 5 g
Sugars 9 g
Protein 51 g
Phosphorus 605 mg

WEDNESDAY NIGHT

FISH CAKES WITH QUICK COLESLAW

SERVES: 4

SERVING SIZE: 5 ounces tilapia, 6 tablespoons mayonnaise and vegetable filling, 1/4 cup coating, 2 ounces whole-wheat baguette, 2 cups coleslaw, 2 tablespoons dressing

PREP TIME: 15 minutes

COOKING TIME: 15 minutes

Use the reserved bronze tilapia to make these fish cakes. The flavor of the bronzed fish along with some scallions, Worcestershire sauce, and mayonnaise make these quick fish cakes extra tasty.

Homemade coleslaw is a breeze to prepare with ready-to-eat sliced coleslaw mix. Bags with different types of slaw cut and ready to use can be found in the produce section of the supermarket.

HELPFUL HINTS:

- Bring fish to room temperature before making it into the fish cakes.

COUNTDOWN:

- Make coleslaw.
- Make fish cakes.

FISH CAKES

1 1/2 pounds bronzed tilapia (saved from Monday night)
4 tablespoons reduced-fat mayonnaise
2 tablespoons Worcestershire sauce
Several drops hot pepper sauce
6 scallions, chopped
4 egg whites
1 cup whole-wheat bread crumbs
Olive oil spray
1 whole-wheat baguette, cut into 4 portions (2 ounces each)

1. In a large bowl, flake the cooked fish with a fork. Add the mayonnaise, Worcestershire sauce, hot pepper sauce, and scallions; mix well. Blend in egg whites. Shape into 4 cakes about 4 inches in diameter each.

2. Place whole-wheat bread crumbs on a plate. Roll fish cakes in crumbs making sure both sides are coated with crumbs.

3. Heat a large nonstick skillet over medium heat. Spray with olive oil spray. Add fish cakes and cook 5 minutes. Turn over and cook 5 more minutes.

4. Place bread in a toaster oven or broiler to warm for a few minutes. Serve fish cakes with coleslaw and bread on the side.

QUICK COLESLAW

4 tablespoons reduced-fat mayonnaise
4 tablespoons distilled white vinegar
Sugar substitute equivalent to 4 teaspoons sugar (such as natural stevia)
1/2 teaspoon freshly ground black pepper
1 cup sliced red onion
4 cups ready-to-eat sliced coleslaw
4 medium tomatoes, sliced

1. Mix mayonnaise, vinegar, sugar substitute, and pepper together in a large bowl.

2. Add onion and coleslaw mix and toss well. Place on 4 plates and arrange sliced tomatoes on the side.

COST OF MEAL PER PERSON
$5.87

PER SERVING

CHOICES/EXCHANGES
2 1/2 starch, 2 nonstarchy vegetable, 5 lean protein, 2 1/2 fat

Total Calories 570
Total Fat 23 g
Saturated Fat 4.2 g
Monounsaturated Fat 7.9 g
Trans Fat 0.0 g
Cholesterol 85 mg
Sodium 670 mg
Potassium 965 mg
Total Carbohydrate 48 g
Fiber 8 g
Sugars 13 g
Protein 46 g
Phosphorus 135 mg

THURSDAY NIGHT

SLOPPY JOES WITH SALAD

SERVES: 4
SERVING SIZE: 5 ounces ground beef, 1 cup vegetables, 1 cup sauce, 1 whole-wheat roll (2 ounces), 2 1/2 cups salad, 2 tablespoons dressing
PREP TIME: 10 minutes
COOKING TIME: 30 minutes

Sloppy Joes, ground meat in tomato sauce served over bread, has been an American favorite for over half a century.

There are many different claims to the origins of Sloppy Joes. But my favorite story is that Sloppy Joe's restaurant in Key West, Florida, took the Cuban stewed ground meat dish Picadillo—which is traditionally served with rice or potatoes—and served it over 2 halves of Cuban bread and called it a Sloppy Joe.

HELPFUL HINTS:

- Ground buffalo can be used instead of beef.
- Look for a tomato sauce that is low in salt and does not have added sugar.

COUNTDOWN:

- Preheat oven to 350°F for bread.
- Start sauce.
- Toast bread in oven.
- Complete sauce.
- Make salad.

SLOPPY JOES

2 teaspoons canola oil
2 cups diced onion
4 cloves garlic, crushed
2 cups diced green bell pepper
1 1/2 pounds 95%lean ground beef
3 1/2 cups low-sodium, no-sugar-added canned tomato sauce*
4 tablespoons reduced-sodium Worcestershire sauce
4 tablespoons distilled white vinegar
1/4 teaspoon salt
1/4 teaspoons freshly ground black pepper
4 whole-wheat kaiser rolls (2 ounces each)
Olive oil spray

1. Preheat oven to 350°F.

2. Heat the oil in a large nonstick skillet over medium-high heat and add the onions. Sauté until the onions are golden, but not black, about 3 minutes. Add the garlic and green pepper and sauté 5 minutes.

3. Add the ground beef and break it up into small pieces with the cooking spoon as it browns. Lower the heat to medium and add the tomato sauce and mix well. Add the Worcestershire and vinegar and cook gently, stirring occasionally, until the meat is cooked through and flavors are blended, about 15 minutes. Sprinkle with salt and pepper.

4. Cut rolls in half and spray the cut sides with vegetable oil spray. Place in oven for 5 minutes or until golden. Remove and place two halves, cut side up, on each of 4 plates.

5. When sauce is finished, taste for seasoning. Add more vinegar and Worcestershire sauce, if necessary. Spoon meat and sauce over rolls and serve as an open-faced sandwich.

**Look for low-sodium tomato sauce, containing per cup (8 ounces): 103 calories, 0.5 g fat, 21.3 g carbohydrate, 21 mg sodium.*

SALAD

8 cups washed, ready-to-eat romaine lettuce
2 large tomatoes, cut into wedges
8 tablespoons reduced-fat oil and vinegar dressing**

1. Cut lettuce into bite-size pieces. Place lettuce in a bowl with the tomatoes and toss with dressing.

*** Look for reduced-fat oil and vinegar dressing containing per tablespoon: 11 calories, 1.0 g fat, 4 mg sodium.*

COST OF MEAL
PER PERSON
$4.95

PER SERVING

CHOICES/EXCHANGES
2 starch, 6 nonstarchy vegetable, 4 lean protein, 2 fat

Total Calories 580
Total Fat 15 g
Saturated Fat 4.7 g
Monounsaturated Fat 6.6 g
Trans Fat 0.0 g
Cholesterol 110 mg
Sodium 580 mg
Potassium 2230 mg
Total Carbohydrate 61 g
Fiber 12 g
Sugars 25 g
Protein 47 g
Phosphorus 630 mg

FRIDAY NIGHT

PASTA PRIMAVERA

SERVES: 4
SERVING SIZE: 2 cups vegetables, 1/4 cup walnuts, 3/4 cup linguine, 2 tablespoons cheese
PREP TIME: 10 minutes
COOKING TIME: 20 minutes

This is a light meal of pasta and fresh vegetables. You can substitute any fresh vegetables left over from this week's dinners for the bell peppers, tomatoes, and mushrooms in this recipe. Use this recipe as a blueprint for the quantities.

HELPFUL HINTS:

- Any type of whole-wheat pasta can be used in this recipe.

COUNTDOWN:

- Place water for pasta onto boil.
- Sauté vegetables in a skillet.
- When water comes to a boil, add the pasta.
- Toast the walnuts.
- Assemble the dish.

PASTA PRIMAVERA

1/2 pound whole-wheat linguine
1/4 cup olive oil
3/4 cup diced red onion
2 teaspoons minced garlic
2 cups sliced red bell pepper
2 cups sliced button mushrooms
3 plum tomatoes, cut into 1–2-inch pieces (1 1/2 cups)
1 cup walnuts
6 scallions, sliced
1 cup basil leaves, torn into small pieces
1/2 teaspoon salt
1/2 teaspoon freshly ground black pepper
1/2 cup freshly grated Parmesan cheese

1. Fill a large saucepan with 3–4 quarts water and bring to a boil. Stir in the linguine. Cook 8 minutes or until the pasta is tender but still firm. Add 1/4 cup pasta water to a large bowl. Drain pasta and add it to the bowl.

2. Meanwhile, heat oil in a large skillet over medium-high heat and add the onion, garlic, red bell pepper, mushrooms, and tomatoes. Sauté 5 minutes.

3. Toast walnuts in a toaster oven or under a broiler for 2–3 minutes. Do not let them burn.

4. Add the pasta to the skillet and toss well. Add the scallions, basil leaves, salt, and pepper. Toss to combine. Serve on 4 dinner plates and sprinkle with Parmesan cheese and toasted walnuts.

COST OF MEAL
PER PERSON
$3.48

PER SERVING

CHOICES/EXCHANGES
2 1/2 starch, 1/2 carbohydrate,
2 nonstarchy vegetable,
1 high-fat protein, 5 fat

Total Calories 620
Total Fat 37 g
Saturated Fat 4.9 g
Monounsaturated Fat 12.3 g
Trans Fat 0.0 g
Cholesterol 10 mg
Sodium 490 mg
Potassium 935 mg
Total Carbohydrate 58 g
Fiber 11 g
Sugars 8 g
Protein 22 g
Phosphorus 500 mg

SATURDAY NIGHT

FIVE-SPICE CHICKEN WITH CHINESE NOODLES

SERVES: 4

SERVING SIZE: 5 ounces chicken, 3/4 cup cooked vegetables, 1/2 cup sauce, 3/4 cup noodles, 1/4 cup scallions

PREP TIME: 10 minutes

COOKING TIME: 10 minutes

The pungent flavors of Chinese five-spice powder, rice vinegar, and soy sauce combine to create this sweet and savory chicken dinner. Chinese five-spice powder is used in many Asian dishes and is a blend of cinnamon, cloves, fennel seed, star anise, and Szechuan peppercorns. It can be found in the spice section of the supermarket.

HELPFUL HINTS:

- White vinegar diluted with a little water can be used instead of rice vinegar.
- A wok or skillet can be used to make the chicken.
- Dried Chinese noodles or angel hair pasta can be used instead of fresh Chinese noodles.
- The quickest way to slice scallions is to snip them with a scissors.

COUNTDOWN:

- Place water for noodles on to boil.
- Make chicken.
- Boil noodles.

FIVE-SPICE CHICKEN

1/2 cup water
3/4 cup Chinese rice vinegar
8 teaspoons Chinese five-spice powder
8 teaspoons minced garlic
3 tablespoons reduced-sodium soy sauce
12 teaspoons sesame oil, divided
1/2 pound broccoli, cut into 1-inch pieces (about 3 cups)
1 1/2 pounds boneless, skinless chicken breasts, cut into 1/2-inch pieces

1. Mix water, rice vinegar, Chinese five-spice, garlic, soy sauce, and 4 teaspoons sesame oil together in a bowl. Set aside.

2. Heat remaining 8 teaspoons sesame oil over high heat in a large wok or skillet until smoking. Add broccoli and stir-fry 2 minutes. Add chicken and continue to stir-fry 4 minutes. Add sauce and mix in with the chicken and vegetables for 2 minutes.

3. Remove chicken and broccoli to a plate and boil sauce to reduce, about 1 minute. To serve, place chicken on top of noodles and spoon sauce over both.

CHINESE NOODLES

1/2 pound steamed or fresh Chinese noodles
1 tablespoon sesame oil
1/4 teaspoon salt
1/2 teaspoon freshly ground black pepper
1 cup scallions, sliced

1. Fill a large saucepan with 3–4 quarts of water and bring to a boil. Add the fresh noodles. Bring back to a boil.

2. Remove 2 tablespoons cooking water to a large bowl. Add sesame oil to the bowl. Drain noodles. (For dried noodles, cook for 3–4 minutes before draining.)
Add noodles and salt and pepper to the bowl. Toss well. Divide among 4 plates and sprinkle with scallions.

COST OF MEAL PER PERSON
$5.47

PER SERVING

CHOICES/EXCHANGES
2 1/2 starch, 1/2 carbohydrate, 2 nonstarchy vegetable, 6 lean protein, 2 fat

Total Calories 650
Total Fat 25 g
Saturated Fat 4.1 g
Monounsaturated Fat 9.0 g
Trans Fat 0.0 g
Cholesterol 175 mg
Sodium 650 mg
Potassium 965 mg
Total Carbohydrate 54 g
Fiber 5 g
Sugars 3 g
Protein 54 g
Phosphorus 570 mg

WEEK **FIVE**

WEEKLY BUDGET
Average cost of a meal per person for the week is
$3.60

SUNDAY NIGHT
HOT GLAZED PORK CHOPS WITH ARUGULA AND WALNUT SALAD

A tangy and sweet mustard and marmalade glaze coats boneless pork chops, and a peppery salad completes the meal.

MONDAY NIGHT
LEMON DILL SALMON WITH PARSLEY RICE

Refreshing lemon and olive oil is all that is needed to dress fresh wild salmon. Rice topped with fresh parsley completes the meal. Half the salmon is wrapped and refrigerated for Wednesday night's dinner.

TUESDAY NIGHT
SMOKY PAN-ROASTED CHICKEN WITH POTATOES AND GREEN BEANS

Smoked paprika, cumin, and honey flavor this chicken. Half of the chicken is saved for a quick Thursday night dinner. Potatoes and green beans are cooked together for the side dish.

WEDNESDAY NIGHT
LEMON PEPPER SALMON AND LINGUINE WITH ITALIAN SALAD

This meal can be made in the time it takes to boil the linguine. It uses the reserved cooked salmon from Monday night to make preparing the meal quick and easy. Washed, ready-to-eat romaine lettuce and arugula make a peppery salad.

THURSDAY NIGHT
SMOKY CHICKEN AND THREE BEAN SALAD

This Southwestern salad uses the reserved cooked chicken from Tuesday's dinner. A toasted baguette with melted Parmesan cheese complements the smoky flavors of the salad.

FRIDAY NIGHT
ONION, TOMATO, AND PARMESAN FRITTATA

This light vegetarian frittata uses some of the remaining vegetables and herbs from this week's shopping list. It's a simple and comforting Friday night family dinner.

SATURDAY NIGHT
PEANUT-CRUSTED PORK WITH MIXED VEGETABLE KABOBS AND CORN ON THE COB

Fire up the grill or use your stove-top indoors to make these grilled kabobs and spicy corn on the cob!

SHOPPING LIST

SHOP SMART

- Low-sodium diced tomatoes containing per cup: 41 calories, 9.6 g carbohydrate, 24 mg sodium.
- Look for reduced-fat oil and vinegar dressing containing per tablespoon: 11 calories, 1.0 g fat, 4 mg sodium.

Here is the Shopping List for this week's dinners.

This shopping list will help you get in and out of the market quickly. The ingredients are listed by supermarket department to make shopping easier; you won't forget something in one department and have to go back and forth across the store.

The amount needed of each ingredient is listed so you will know what size package or can to buy. If it helps you to better visualize the amount you need, please note that 4 tablespoons equal 1/4 cup and 8 tablespoons equal 1/2 cup.

Make sure to check your refrigerator and pantry to see if you have any of these ingredients on hand before making your trip to the market.

MEAT AND SEAFOOD

3 pounds boneless pork chops (1/2 inch thick)
3 pounds wild-caught salmon fillets
3 pounds boneless, skinless chicken thighs

DAIRY

14 large eggs
1 small piece Parmesan cheese
(1/4 cup plus 6 tablespoons grated needed)

BAKERY

2 whole-wheat baguettes (12 ounces each)
1 small package whole-wheat croutons (2 cups needed)

CONDIMENTS

1 small bottle hot pepper sauce
1 small jar Dijon mustard (1 tablespoon needed)

PASTA AND RICE

1/2 pound fresh whole-wheat linguine
Microwaveable brown rice (to make 3 cups cooked rice)

CANNED VEGETABLES

1 can low-sodium chickpeas (3/4 cup needed)
1 can low-sodium red kidney beans (1 cup needed)
1 large can low-sodium diced tomatoes (2 cups needed) (see *Shop Smart*, opposite)

SPICE SECTION

1 bottle smoked paprika (4 teaspoons needed)
1 bottle ground cumin (4 teaspoons needed)
1 small bottle cracked black pepper (2 teaspoons needed)

JAM AND HONEY

1 small bottle honey (4 tablespoons needed)
1 small jar hot pepper jam (6 tablespoons needed)
1 small jar orange marmalade (6 tablespoons needed)

NUTS

1 small package walnut pieces (1 cup needed)
1 small package dry-roasted, unsalted peanuts (1/4 cup needed)

PRODUCE

2 onions (2 cups needed)
4 medium red bell peppers (4 cups needed)
3/4 pound portobello mushrooms (4 cups needed)
4 lemons (5 tablespoons needed)
2 pounds red or yellow potatoes
1 1/2 pounds trimmed green beans
4 ears corn on the cob
1 large package arugula (10 cups needed)
1 package washed, ready-to-eat romaine lettuce (8 cups needed)
1 large bunch fresh dill (11 tablespoons needed)
1 large bunch fresh parsley (1 cup needed)
1 bunch cilantro (1/2 cup needed)
1 1/4 pounds asparagus

STAPLES

Olive oil
Olive oil spray
Reduced-fat oil and vinegar dressing (see *Shop Smart*, opposite)
Salt
Black peppercorns

SUNDAY NIGHT

HOT GLAZED PORK CHOPS WITH ARUGULA AND WALNUT SALAD

SERVES: 4
SERVING SIZE: 5 ounces pork chop, 2 tablespoons sauce, 2 cups salad, 1/2 cup croutons, 1/4 cup walnuts, 1 tablespoon dressing
PREP TIME: 10 minutes
COOKING TIME: 10 minutes

Dijon mustard and orange marmalade create a spicy, sweet glaze for quick-cooking boneless pork chops. The secret to speedy cooking is to buy thin-cut pork chops or cut thicker ones in half horizontally to make a 1/2-inch-thick chop. Half the pork chops are used for this dinner. The remaining half should be used for Saturday night's dinner.

Peppery arugula and walnuts make a crunchy salad to complete this meal.

HELPFUL HINTS:

- Pecans or almonds can be used instead of walnuts.
- Any type of croutons can be used for the salad.

COUNTDOWN:

- Prepare all ingredients.
- Start pork chops.
- While pork chops cook, assemble salad.

HOT GLAZED PORK CHOPS

6 tablespoons orange marmalade
1 tablespoon Dijon mustard
Several drops hot pepper sauce
1 1/2 pounds thin-cut boneless pork chops (1/2 inch thick)
2 teaspoons olive oil
1/2 teaspoon salt
1/2 teaspoon freshly ground black pepper

1. Mix together marmalade and mustard in a small bowl. Add a few drops of hot pepper sauce. Set aside.

2. Remove visible fat from pork chops. Heat oil in a large nonstick skillet over medium-high heat.

3. Add pork chops and sauté 3 minutes. Turn, cover with a lid, and cook 2 more minutes. A meat thermometer inserted into pork should read 145°F. Sprinkle with salt and pepper and transfer to individual dinner plates.

4. Add marmalade mixture to the skillet and sauté for 30 seconds or until marmalade melts, scraping up any brown bits in the pan. Spoon sauce over pork and serve.

ARUGULA AND WALNUT SALAD

8 cups washed, ready-to-eat arugula
1 cup coarsely chopped walnuts
1/4 cup reduced-fat oil and vinegar dressing
2 cups whole-wheat croutons (about 4 ounces)

1. Divide the arugula among 4 plates. Add the walnuts. Drizzle the salad with the dressing and sprinkle croutons on top.

COST OF MEAL PER PERSON

$3.57

PER SERVING

CHOICES/EXCHANGES
1 starch, 1 carbohydrate, 1 nonstarchy vegetable, 6 lean protein, 3 fat

Total Calories 580
Total Fat 27 g
Saturated Fat 3.0 g
Monounsaturated Fat 7.6 g
Trans Fat 0.0 g
Cholesterol 95 mg
Sodium 580 mg
Potassium 1085 mg
Total Carbohydrate 37 g
Fiber 5 g
Sugars 21 g
Protein 52 g
Phosphorus 635 mg

MONDAY NIGHT

LEMON DILL SALMON WITH PARSLEY RICE

SERVES: 4
SERVING SIZE: 5 ounces salmon, 3/4 cup rice, 1 cup cooked vegetables, 2 tablespoons parsley
PREP TIME: 10 minutes
COOKING TIME: 15 minutes

Wild salmon is so flavorful! It only needs a little olive oil, lemon juice, and salt and pepper. Salmon is available fresh from mid-May until mid-September. At other times of the year, good-quality wild salmon can be found in the frozen seafood section of the supermarket. King salmon (also called Chinook), Coho, and sockeye are some of the wild salmon varieties to look for.

For this recipe, 3 pounds of salmon fillets are cooked and half of the salmon is saved and refrigerated for Wednesday night's dinner.

HELPFUL HINTS:

- If you can't find wild salmon, farmed salmon can be used for this recipe, but the flavor will be different.
- A quick way to chop dill and parsley is to wash and dry the herbs and then snip the leaves right off the stem with a scissors.

COUNTDOWN:

- Preheat oven to 425°F.
- Prepare and bake salmon.
- Make rice while salmon bakes.

LEMON DILL SALMON

Olive oil spray
3 pounds wild-caught salmon fillets (half saved for Wednesday night's dinner)
1 teaspoon salt
1/2 teaspoon freshly ground black pepper
3 tablespoons lemon juice
3 tablespoons chopped fresh dill OR 3 teaspoons dried dill

1. Preheat oven to 425°F. Line a baking sheet with foil and spray with olive oil spray.

2. Place salmon, skin side down, on the baking sheet. Spray salmon with olive oil spray. Place on middle rack in oven for 15 minutes or until salmon is just cooked through. When a knife is inserted into the fish, the flesh should be opaque, not translucent. (Do not overcook; the salmon will continue to cook in its own heat when salmon is out of the oven.)

3. Remove from oven and sprinkle salmon with salt and pepper. Set half of the salmon aside and refrigerate for Wednesday's dinner. Spoon lemon juice over the remaining salmon and sprinkle with dill. Serve with the rice.

PARSLEY RICE

Microwaveable brown rice (to make 3 cups cooked)
1 1/4 pounds asparagus (4 cups sliced)
4 teaspoons olive oil
1/2 cup chopped parsley
1/2 teaspoon salt
1/4 teaspoon freshly ground black pepper

1. Microwave rice according to package instructions. Measure 3 cups rice and reserve any remaining rice for another time.

2. Trim 1 inch off the bottom of the asparagus and discard. Cut asparagus into 1-inch pieces. Place in a microwave-safe bowl and microwave on high 4 minutes.

3. Remove from the microwave and add the rice, oil, parsley, and salt and pepper. Toss well.

COST OF MEAL
PER PERSON
$5.70

PER SERVING

CHOICES/EXCHANGES
2 1/2 starch, 2 nonstarchy vegetable, 4 lean protein, 2 fat

Total Calories 520
Total Fat 19 g
Saturated Fat 2.9 g
Monounsaturated Fat 7.7 g
Trans Fat 0.0 g
Cholesterol 95 mg
Sodium 670 mg
Potassium 1025 mg
Total Carbohydrate 46 g
Fiber 6 g
Sugars 3 g
Protein 41 g
Phosphorus 505 mg

TUESDAY NIGHT

SMOKY PAN-ROASTED CHICKEN WITH POTATOES AND GREEN BEANS

SERVES: 4

SERVING SIZE: 5 ounces chicken, 1 tablespoon sauce, 1 1/2 cups potatoes, 1 cup green beans, 1 1/2 teaspoons oil

PREP TIME: 10 minutes

COOKING TIME: 20 minutes

Smoked paprika gives this pan-roasted chicken a delicious smoky flavor. This recipe calls for cooking 3 pounds of chicken. Once cooked, half of the chicken is saved for Thursday night's dinner.

HELPFUL HINTS:

- Save yourself some preparation time; buy trimmed beans from the produce section of the market.
- Smoked paprika can be found in the spice section of the supermarket.
- Use two skillets if you don't have one that will fit all of the chicken.

COUNTDOWN:

- Start potatoes.
- Make the chicken.
- Finish the potatoes and beans.

SMOKY PAN-ROASTED CHICKEN

4 teaspoons ground smoked paprika
4 teaspoons ground cumin
4 tablespoons honey
3 pounds boneless, skinless chicken thighs
Olive oil spray
1/2 cup chopped cilantro

1. In a small bowl mix the smoked paprika, cumin, and honey together until smooth. It will be a thick paste.

2. Remove visible fat from the chicken. Heat a large nonstick skillet over medium-high heat. Spray with olive oil spray. Add chicken, smooth side down. Brown 2 minutes. Turn and brown 2 more minutes.

3. Spoon honey mixture over chicken. Cover skillet with a lid, lower heat to medium, and cook 5 minutes. A meat thermometer inserted into chicken should read 170°F.

4. Remove chicken from stove. Set aside half the chicken and refrigerate for Thursday night's dinner. Divide remaining chicken among 4 plates and sprinkle with cilantro.

POTATOES AND GREEN BEANS

2 pounds red or yellow potatoes, washed and cut into 1-inch pieces
1 pound trimmed green beans, cut into 1-inch pieces (about 4 cups)
2 tablespoons olive oil
1/2 teaspoon salt
1/4 teaspoon freshly ground black pepper

1. Place potatoes in a large saucepan and fill with cold water to cover potatoes. Cover pan with a lid and bring to a boil. Boil, gently, for 10 minutes.

2. Add the green beans to the pan and continue to boil, uncovered, 5 minutes or until the potatoes are cooked through. Drain vegetables, place in a bowl, and toss with oil, salt, and pepper.

COST OF MEAL PER PERSON

$2.35

PER SERVING

CHOICES/EXCHANGES
2 1/2 starch, 1/2 carbohydrate, 2 nonstarchy vegetable, 4 lean protein, 1 1/2 fat

Total Calories 520
Total Fat 17 g
Saturated Fat 3.2 g
Monounsaturated fat 7.1 g
Trans Fat 0.0 g
Cholesterol 140 mg
Sodium 490 mg
Potassium 1705 mg
Total Carbohydrate 54 g
Fiber 7 g
Sugars 15 g
Protein 41 g
Phosphorus 465 mg

WEDNESDAY NIGHT

LEMON PEPPER SALMON AND LINGUINE WITH ITALIAN SALAD

SERVES: 4
SERVING SIZE: 3/4 cup cooked pasta, 5 ounces salmon, 1 teaspoon olive oil, 1 1/2 cups salad, 1 tablespoon dressing
PREP TIME: 10 minutes
COOKING TIME: 10 minutes

You can make this meal in the time it takes to cook the pasta. It uses the extra cooked salmon from Monday night's dinner. Mix arugula with romaine lettuce for a quick, Italian-style salad.

HELPFUL HINTS:

- Dried linguine can be used instead of fresh. Boil it 8–10 minutes or according to package instructions.
- Cracked black pepper can be found in the spice section of the market.

COUNTDOWN:

- Place water for pasta on to boil.
- Assemble salad.
- Cook pasta and complete recipe.

LEMON PEPPER SALMON AND LINGUINE

1/2 pound fresh whole-wheat linguine
4 teaspoons olive oil
2 teaspoons cracked black pepper
2 tablespoons lemon juice
1 1/4 pounds lemon dill salmon (saved from Monday night), cut into 1-inch pieces
1/2 teaspoon salt

1. Fill a large saucepan with water and bring to a boil. Add the linguine and boil 4–5 minutes or according to package instructions.

2. Remove 3 tablespoons linguine cooking water to a large bowl. Add the olive oil, cracked black pepper, and lemon juice to the bowl.

3. Drain linguine and add to the bowl. Toss well. Add the salmon and salt and gently toss again. Divide among 4 plates.

See p. 87, following photo insert, for Italian Salad

Shrimp and Avocado Tartine with Watercress Salad p. 100–101

Spiced Lamb Steak with Florentine Rice p. 146–147

Spaghetti and Meatballs p. 10–11

Salmon Burgers with Sautéed Broccoli Raab p. 208–209

Garlic Steak and Linguine with Shredded Carrots p. 188–189

Shrimp and Mushroom Pizza p. 56–57

Panzanella Salad (Tuscan Tomato and Bread Salad) p. 176–177

Cajun Chicken with Rice and Red Beans p. 200–201

ITALIAN SALAD

4 cups washed ready-to-eat romaine lettuce
2 cups arugula
4 tablespoons reduced-fat salad dressing

1. Add lettuce and arugula to a salad bowl and toss with the dressing.

See p. 86, preceding photo insert, for Lemon Pepper Salmon and Linguine

COST OF MEAL PER PERSON
$4.20

PER SERVING

CHOICES/EXCHANGES
2 1/2 starch, 1 nonstarchy vegetable, 5 lean protein, 1 1/2 fat

Total Calories 510
Total Fat 17 g
Saturated Fat 2.7 g
Monounsaturated Fat 6.3 g
Trans Fat 0.0 g
Cholesterol 95 mg
Sodium 670 mg
Potassium 1270 mg
Total Carbohydrate 46 g
Fiber 7 g
Sugars 3 g
Protein 43 g
Phosphorus 560 mg

THURSDAY NIGHT

SMOKY CHICKEN AND THREE BEAN SALAD

SERVES: 4
SERVING SIZE: 3 ounces whole-wheat baguette, 1 tablespoon Parmesan cheese, 5 ounces cooked chicken, 2 cups salad, 1 tablespoon dressing
PREP TIME: 10 minutes
COOKING TIME: 5 minutes

Roasted chicken from Tuesday night is used in this Southwestern salad dinner. A toasted baguette with Parmesan cheese complements this tasty chicken and bean salad.

Trimmed green beans help make preparation for this dinner quick and easy.

HELPFUL HINTS:

- Toast baguette with cheese in a toaster oven or under a broiler.
- Use the same bowl for microwaving green beans and making the salad.

COUNTDOWN:

- Toast baguette.
- Make salad.

SMOKY CHICKEN AND THREE BEAN SALAD

1 whole-wheat baguette (12 ounces total)
1/4 cup freshly grated Parmesan cheese
1/2 pound trimmed green beans, cut into 1-inch pieces (about 2 cups)
1 1/4 pounds smoky pan-roasted chicken (saved from Tuesday night), cut into 1-inch-thick strips
3/4 cup rinsed and drained, low-sodium canned chickpeas
1 cup rinsed and drained, low-sodium canned red kidney beans
1/4 cup reduced-fat oil and vinegar dressing*
1/4 teaspoon freshly ground black pepper
4 cups romaine lettuce

1. Slice baguette in half lengthwise and then in half horizontally to make 4 pieces. Sprinkle the inside with Parmesan cheese and place in toaster oven to melt cheese, about 2 minutes.

2. Place green beans in a large microwave-safe bowl and microwave on high 2 minutes.

3. Remove from microwave and add chicken, chickpeas, red kidney beans, and dressing. Toss well. Add pepper and toss again.

4. Divide lettuce among 4 dinner plates. Divide salad into 4 servings and spoon over lettuce. Serve with Parmesan baguettes.

**Look for reduced-fat oil and vinegar dressing containing per tablespoon: 11 calories, 1.0 g fat, 4 mg sodium.*

COST OF MEAL
PER PERSON
$2.63

PER SERVING

CHOICES/EXCHANGES
3 starch, 2 nonstarchy vegetable, 5 lean protein, 1 fat

Total Calories 550
Total Fat 15 g
Saturated Fat 3.3 g
Monounsaturated Fat 5.3 g
Trans Fat 0.0 g
Cholesterol 145 mg
Sodium 590 mg
Potassium 755 mg
Total Carbohydrate 58 g
Fiber 8 g
Sugars 14 g
Protein 46 g
Phosphorus 400 mg

FRIDAY NIGHT

ONION, TOMATO, AND PARMESAN FRITTATA

SERVES: 4
SERVING SIZE: 1 1/2 eggs, 2 egg whites, 1 1/4 cups vegetables, 1 1/2 tablespoons cheese, 3 ounces whole-wheat baguette
PREP TIME: 10 minutes
COOKING TIME: 25 minutes

Enjoy this light, vegetarian frittata that uses vegetables and herbs from the week's grocery list. Frittatas and omelets are different things. A frittata is cooked very slowly over low heat making it firm and set, while an omelet is cooked fast over high heat making it creamy and runny. A frittata needs to be cooked on both sides. Some people flip it in the pan, but a much easier technique is to place it under a broiler for a minute.

This recipe serves 4 and is cooked in two batches. To save time, it can be made in 2 skillets at once.

HELPFUL HINTS:

- A quick way to chop dill and parsley is to wash and dry the herbs and then snip the leaves with a scissors right off the stem.
- Toast baguette with cheese in a toaster oven or under a broiler.
- Use an ovenproof skillet that can go under the broiler.

COUNTDOWN:

- Preheat broiler.
- Make frittata.
- While frittata cooks, make toast.

ONION, TOMATO, AND PARMESAN FRITTATA

2 cups thinly sliced onion
2 cups drained, low-sodium canned diced tomatoes
1/2 cup fresh dill leaves, torn into bite-size pieces
1/2 cup chopped parsley leaves
6 whole eggs
8 egg whites
6 tablespoons freshly grated Parmesan cheese
1/4 teaspoon freshly ground black pepper
Olive oil spray
1 whole-wheat baguette (12 ounces total), cut into 4 pieces

1. Preheat broiler.

2. Place onion and tomatoes in a microwave-safe bowl. Microwave on high 5 minutes. Remove from microwave and add dill and parsley.

3. Mix whole eggs and egg whites together in a large bowl. Add Parmesan cheese, onion and tomato mixture, and pepper.

4. Heat a 9-inch nonstick skillet over medium-low heat. Spray with olive oil spray and add half the egg mixture. Reduce the heat to low. Cook without browning the bottom for 10 minutes. The eggs will be set, but the top will be a little runny.

5. Place pan under the broiler for 1 minute until the top is set but not brown. Remove frittata from pan and cut in half. Slide halves onto 2 plates.

6. Repeat steps 4 and 5 with the second half of the egg mixture.

7. Toast bread and spray one side of each piece with olive oil spray. Serve frittata with 1 piece of toast per person.

COST OF MEAL PER PERSON

$2.17

PER SERVING

CHOICES/EXCHANGES
2 starch, 2 nonstarchy vegetable, 2 lean protein, 2 fat

Total Calories 390
Total Fat 13 g
Saturated Fat 4.0 g
Monounsaturated Fat 5.3 g
Trans Fat 0.0 g
Cholesterol 285 mg
Sodium 640 mg
Potassium 590 mg
Total Carbohydrate 42 g
Fiber 6 g
Sugars 6 g
Protein 26 g
Phosphorus 245 mg

SATURDAY NIGHT

PEANUT-CRUSTED PORK WITH MIXED VEGETABLE KABOBS AND CORN ON THE COB

SERVES: 4
SERVING SIZE: 5 ounces pork, 1 1/2 tablespoons jelly, 1 tablespoon peanuts, 2 cups vegetables, 1 ear corn
PREP TIME: 20 minutes
COOKING TIME: 15 minutes

Finish out your week with this sweet and spicy pork dish! Peanuts and hot pepper jelly coat juicy pork cubes in this barbecue dinner. Mushrooms, red bell pepper, and corn on the cob complete the meal.

I find that the meat and vegetables take different times to cook. To solve this problem, I thread the meat onto one skewer and the vegetables onto another. Each skewer can be removed from the heat when ready, so you won't have to overcook the meat while the vegetables finish cooking.

HELPFUL HINTS:

- Green bell pepper can be used instead of red bell pepper.
- Any type of mushroom can be used.
- To help the cubes of meat cook evenly on a skewer, I leave at least 1/4 inch of space between them. That way the heat can reach the sides of the food as well as the top and bottom. Use more skewers if needed.
- Chop the peanuts using a food processor.
- A stove-top grill or broiler can be used for this dinner instead of a grill.

COUNTDOWN:

- Prepare the ingredients.
- Heat the grill.
- Make the kabobs and corn.

PEANUT-CRUSTED PORK WITH MIXED VEGETABLE KABOBS AND CORN ON THE COB

6 tablespoons hot pepper jelly, divided
1 1/2 pounds boneless pork chops, visible fat removed and cut into 1 1/2-inch cubes
4 tablespoons chopped, dry-roasted, unsalted peanuts
8 metal skewers
4 cups chopped (1-inch pieces) red bell pepper (about 4 medium peppers)
3/4 pound portobello mushrooms, cut into 1-inch pieces (about 4 cups)
Olive oil spray
2 large squares foil (about 12 inches each)
4 medium ears corn on the cob, husked

1. Preheat grill to medium heat.

2. Place 2 tablespoons jelly in a bowl and stir to make it smooth. Toss meat in the jelly and then roll in chopped peanuts. Thread meat onto 4 of the skewers.

3. Place red bell pepper and mushrooms in a microwave-safe bowl and microwave on high 3 minutes. Remove from microwave and thread vegetables onto 4 skewers alternating peppers and mushrooms. Spray with olive oil spray.

4. Spoon remaining jelly onto the foil squares. Place 2 ears of corn on each piece of foil and roll in the jelly. Close foil and seal the corn inside.

5. Place pork skewers on the grill and cook 3 minutes. Turn and grill another 3 minutes. A meat thermometer inserted into pork should read 145°F.

6. At the same time, place corn and vegetables on the grill and grill 5 minutes. Turn corn and skewers and grill another 5 minutes. Remove from grill and serve with the pork.

COST OF MEAL
PER PERSON
$4.54

PER SERVING

CHOICES/EXCHANGES
1 1/2 starch, 1/2 carbohydrate, 2 nonstarchy vegetable, 5 lean protein, 1 fat

Total Calories 460
Total Fat 14 g
Saturated Fat 2.4 g
Monounsaturated Fat 5.7 g
Trans Fat 0.0 g
Cholesterol 95 mg
Sodium 180 mg
Potassium 1395 mg
Total Carbohydrate 41 g
Fiber 6 g
Sugars 21 g
Protein 49 g
Phosphorus 575 mg

WEEK **SIX**

WEEKLY BUDGET
Average cost of a meal per person for the week is
$7.15

SUNDAY NIGHT

MEDITERRANEAN STEAK WITH MINTED COUSCOUS

Pan-seared steak topped with walnuts, olives, and capers captures the flavor of the Mediterranean. Couscous with mint and tomatoes completes the meal. Extra steak is sautéed for a quick steak sandwich on Wednesday night.

MONDAY NIGHT

SHRIMP AND AVOCADO TARTINE WITH WATERCRESS SALAD

Grilled shrimp, creamy avocado, and pesto sauce top a slice of bread for a quick sandwich supper. Peppery watercress makes a tasty side salad.

TUESDAY NIGHT

COUNTRY MUSHROOM AND SAUSAGE SOUP

This comforting bowl of soup can be made in just 20 minutes. It's filled with turkey sausage, mushrooms, and beans—a real family-pleasing meal in a bowl.

WEDNESDAY NIGHT

STEAK AND PORTOBELLO SANDWICH WITH TAPENADE-TOPPED TOMATOES

Balsamic dipping sauce, meaty portobello mushrooms, and reserved steak from Sunday night make a tasty supper. Tapenade made with olives, capers, oil, and vinegar make a special topping for fresh sliced tomatoes.

THURSDAY NIGHT

HOT AND SPICY STIR-FRY SHRIMP AND SESAME NOODLES WITH SNOW PEAS

These spicy shrimp are stir-fried with hot pepper sauce, garlic, and ginger. Sesame oil adds a nutty flavor to the shrimp and the Chinese noodles, which are stir-fried with crisp snow peas.

FRIDAY NIGHT

WALNUT AND FENNEL PASTA

Toasted walnuts, crisp fennel, and diced tomatoes give this light vegetarian dish a crunchy texture and an anise or licorice flavor.

SATURDAY NIGHT

TURKEY PESTO WRAP WITH PARMESAN CAULIFLOWER

Wrap turkey slices with pesto sauce and watercress in a tortilla and serve the wrap with a side of cauliflower tossed with Parmesan cheese and bread crumbs for an amazing, easy dinner.

SHOPPING LIST

Here is the Shopping List for this week's dinners.

This shopping list will help you get in and out of the market quickly. The ingredients are listed by supermarket department to make shopping easier; you won't forget something in one department and have to go back and forth across the store.

The amount needed of each ingredient is listed so you will know what size package or can to buy. If it helps you to better visualize the amount you need, please note that 4 tablespoons equal 1/4 cup and 8 tablespoons equal 1/2 cup.

Make sure to check your refrigerator and pantry to see if you have any of these ingredients on hand before making your trip to the market.

MEAT AND SEAFOOD
3 pounds grass-fed steak (strip, flank, or skirt)
3/4 pound low-fat turkey sausage
3 pounds frozen, shelled large shrimp (wild caught or local)

DAIRY
1 small piece Parmesan cheese (6 tablespoons needed)

DELI
1 1/4 pounds sliced no-salt-added deli turkey breast

BAKERY
1 small loaf multigrain or whole-grain bread (8 slices needed)
4 whole-wheat hoagie (submarine) rolls (about 2 ounces each)
1 package 8-inch whole-wheat tortillas (4 needed)

SHOP SMART

- Low-sodium, no-sugar-added pasta sauce containing per cup (8 ounces): 131 calories, 3.8 g fat, 20.7 g carbohydrate, 77 mg sodium.
- Low-sodium diced tomatoes containing per cup: 41 calories, 9.6 g carbohydrate, 24 mg sodium.
- Look for reduced-fat oil and vinegar dressing containing per tablespoon: 11 calories, 1.0 g fat, 4 mg sodium.

CONDIMENTS

1 small jar sliced pimento-stuffed green olives (16 olives needed)
1 small jar capers (3 tablespoons needed)
1 small bottle hot pepper sauce (1 teaspoon needed)
1 small bottle sesame oil (4 teaspoons needed)
1 bottle balsamic vinegar (1 cup needed)
1 jar olive tapenade (4 tablespoons needed)
1 package reduced-fat pesto sauce (8 tablespoons needed)
1 small jar reduced-fat mayonnaise (1 1/2 tablespoons needed)

PASTA, RICE, BREAD CRUMBS

1 package couscous (1 cup needed)
1 package Chinese noodles (8 ounces needed)
1/2 pound whole-wheat spaghetti
1 small package whole-wheat bread crumbs (1/4 cup needed)

CANNED VEGETABLES

1 bottle no-sugar-added, low-sodium pasta sauce (5 1/2 cups needed) (see *Shop Smart*, opposite)
1 can tomato paste (1/2 cup needed)
1 can low-sodium diced tomatoes (2 cups needed) (see *Shop Smart*, opposite)
1 can low-sodium red kidney beans (3/4 cup needed)

SPICE SECTION

1 bottle fennel seeds (2 tablespoons needed)

NUTS AND SEEDS

1 small package broken walnut pieces (1 cup plus 2 tablespoons needed)
1 small jar dry-roasted, unsalted peanuts (4 tablespoons needed)
1 package sesame seeds (2 tablespoons needed)

PRODUCE

3 onions (2 1/2 cups needed)
8 medium tomatoes
1 bunch fresh mint (1/2 cup needed)
2 pounds sliced mushrooms
1/2 pound whole portobello mushrooms
1 piece fresh ginger (1/4 cup needed)
3 lemons
1 pound snow peas
2 ripe avocados (2 cups needed)
2 bunches watercress (5 cups needed)
1 head cauliflower (6 cups needed)
1 fennel bulb (1 1/2 cups needed)

STAPLES

Black peppercorns
Garlic (14 cloves needed)
Olive oil
Olive oil spray
Reduced-fat oil and vinegar dressing (4 tablespoons needed) (see *Shop Smart*, opposite)
Salt
Sugar

SUNDAY NIGHT

MEDITERRANEAN STEAK WITH MINTED COUSCOUS

SERVES: 4
SERVING SIZE: 5 ounces steak, 4 olives, 2 teaspoons capers, 3/4 cup couscous, 3/4 cup tomatoes
PREP TIME: 10 minutes
COOKING TIME: 15 minutes

The flavors of the Mediterranean have captured the imagination of travelers for centuries. Precooked, packaged couscous takes only 5 minutes to make, so it's a great option for a quick dinner. Couscous is made from semolina flour and is, in fact, a form of pasta even though many people think it is a grain. You just boil water, remove it from the heat, add the couscous, cover, and let it stand. For this recipe I've added fresh mint and chopped tomatoes to add a fresh flavor that goes well with the steak.

Cook 3 pounds of steak tonight, but save and refrigerate half for Wednesday night's dinner.

HELPFUL HINTS:

- Use skillets that are just large enough to fit the steak in order to capture the pan juices. A larger skillet will cause the juices to boil off.

COUNTDOWN:

- Prepare all ingredients.
- Bring water for couscous to a boil.
- Make couscous.
- Make steak.

MEDITERRANEAN STEAK

3 pounds grass-fed steak (strip, flank, or skirt)
Olive oil spray
2 tablespoons walnut pieces
16 pimento-stuffed green olives (about 2/3 cup sliced)
3 tablespoons capers
1/4 teaspoon freshly ground black pepper

1. Remove visible fat from steak. Heat 2 large nonstick skillets over medium-high heat. Spray skillets with olive oil spray.

2. Divide the steak into 2 portions so that there is half in one skillet and half in the second skillet. Brown steaks 2 minutes.

3. Turn steak over in both skillets. In one skillet sprinkle walnuts, olives, and capers into the skillet with the steak. Cook steaks on the second side for 2 minutes for a 1/2-inch steak. A meat thermometer inserted into steak should read 135°F. (Cook 2 minutes longer for thicker steaks.) Add pepper.

4. Use the steak with the walnuts, olives, and capers tonight's dinner and store the other steak in the refrigerator for Wednesday night's dinner. To serve, divide steak among 4 dinner plates. Spoon pan juices on top.

MINTED COUSCOUS

2 cups water
1 cup couscous
3 tomatoes, diced (about 3 cups)
1/2 cup chopped fresh mint
2 tablespoons olive oil
1/4 teaspoon salt
1/4 teaspoon freshly ground black pepper

1. Bring water to a boil.

2. Remove boiling water from heat and add couscous. Cover with a lid and let stand 5 minutes.

3. When ready, fluff up with a fork. Add tomatoes, mint, olive oil, and salt and pepper.

COST OF MEAL PER PERSON

$10.11

PER SERVING

CHOICES/EXCHANGES
2 1/2 starch, 1 nonstarchy vegetable, 5 lean protein, 1 1/2 fat

Total Calories 510
Total Fat 18 g
Saturated Fat 3.3 g
Monounsaturated Fat 8.2 g
Trans Fat 0.0 g
Cholesterol 95 mg
Sodium 580 mg
Potassium 1055 mg
Total Carbohydrate 42 g
Fiber 6 g
Sugars 4 g
Protein 48 g
Phosphorus 495 mg

MONDAY NIGHT

SHRIMP AND AVOCADO TARTINE WITH WATERCRESS SALAD

SERVES: 4

SERVING SIZE: 5 ounces shrimp, 1/2 cup avocado, 2 slices whole-grain bread, 1/2 cup tomato, 1 tablespoon pesto sauce, 1 cup watercress, 1 tablespoon dressing

PREP TIME: 10 minutes

COOKING TIME: 10 minutes

Grilled shrimp, avocado, and pesto sauce top a thick slice of whole-grain bread to make this quick and easy sandwich supper. "Tartine" means a slice of bread or piece of toast in French, and also can refer to an open-faced sandwich, usually with an elaborate topping. This dinner uses half the shrimp. The remaining shrimp are used for Thursday night's dinner.

Avocado lends a creamy, nutty flavor to this dish. Look for an avocado that gives slightly to pressure. To ripen an avocado, place it in a brown paper bag in a warm spot in your kitchen. Adding a banana or apple to the bag helps speed ripening. Only refrigerate avocados after they are ripe. They will keep 2–3 days that way.

A peppery, tangy watercress salad completes this meal. Watercress is a source of iron, calcium, and vitamin C.

HELPFUL HINTS:

- Cut the avocado lengthwise until you reach the seed and rotate the knife around it. Open the avocado and remove the seed. Cut each half into quarters and peel away the skin.
- The best way to wash watercress is to place the entire bunch of leaves first into a bowl of water. Swish the leaves to release any grit and remove from the water. Spin dry. Wrap the stems in a damp paper towel and store in a self-seal bag. It will keep for several days this way.
- Substitute 1 cup sliced, sautéed mushrooms if ripe avocado is unavailable.

COUNTDOWN:

- Prepare the ingredients.
- Assemble the sandwich.
- Toss the watercress with the dressing and serve.

SHRIMP AND AVOCADO TARTINE

2 cups diced ripe avocado
3 tablespoons lemon juice
Olive oil spray
1 1/2 pounds frozen, shelled large shrimp, defrosted
1/4 teaspoon salt
1/4 teaspoon freshly ground black pepper
8 slices whole-grain bread
2 tomatoes, sliced
4 tablespoons reduced-fat pesto sauce

1. Prepare avocado and place in a bowl with the lemon juice. Toss to make sure all pieces are coated. Set aside.

2. Heat a large nonstick skillet over medium-high heat and spray with olive oil spray. Add shrimp and cook 3–4 minutes or until they turn pink. Sprinkle with salt and pepper.

3. Toast the bread and divide among 4 dinner plates. Spoon avocado onto each slice of toast. Layer tomato slices over the avocado. Top with the shrimp and spoon pesto sauce over the shrimp.

WATERCRESS SALAD

4 cups watercress
4 tablespoons reduced-fat oil and vinegar dressing*

1. Toss watercress with the dressing and serve salad next to the tartines.

**Look for reduced-fat oil and vinegar dressing containing per tablespoon: 11 calories, 1.0 g fat, 4 mg sodium.*

COST OF MEAL PER PERSON

$7.86

PER SERVING

CHOICES/EXCHANGES
2 starch, 1 nonstarchy vegetable, 5 lean protein, 2 fat

Total Calories 510
Total Fat 21 g
Saturated Fat 3.2 g
Monounsaturated Fat 11.2 g
Trans Fat 0.0 g
Cholesterol 280 mg
Sodium 700 mg
Potassium 1165 mg
Total Carbohydrate 37 g
Fiber 11 g
Sugars 9 g
Protein 46 g
Phosphorus 545 mg

TUESDAY NIGHT

COUNTRY MUSHROOM AND SAUSAGE SOUP

SERVES: 4

SERVING SIZE: 3 ounces sausage, 3 cups mushrooms, 3 tablespoons beans, 2 cups liquid

PREP TIME: 10 minutes

COOKING TIME: 20 minutes

This quick soup can be made in just 20 minutes. Turkey sausage flavored with fennel can be found in many supermarkets. Look for lean, mild or sweet Italian sausage.

HELPFUL HINTS:

- It's best to use a large saucepan or use two pans and divide the ingredients between them.

COUNTDOWN:

- Cook soup.

COUNTRY MUSHROOM AND SAUSAGE SOUP

4 teaspoons olive oil
2 pounds sliced mushrooms
3/4 pound low-fat turkey sausage, sliced 1/2 inch thick
5 1/2 cups no-sugar-added, low-sodium pasta sauce*
3 cups water
3/4 cup rinsed and drained low-sodium canned red kidney beans
1/4 teaspoon freshly ground black pepper

1. Heat olive oil in a large saucepan over medium-high heat. Add mushrooms and sausage and sauté 5 minutes.

2. Add the pasta sauce, water, and beans. Bring to a simmer over medium heat, cover, and simmer 15 minutes. Add pepper and serve.

**Look for low-sodium pasta sauce containing per 1/2 cup: 112 calories, 3.5 g fat, 17.7 g carbohydrate, 39 mg sodium.*

COST OF MEAL
PER PERSON
$4.89

PER SERVING

CHOICES/EXCHANGES
3 starch, 2 nonstarchy vegetable,
3 lean protein, 1 fat

Total Calories 490
Total Fat 12 g
Saturated Fat 2.2 g
Monounsaturated Fat 6.4 g
Trans Fat 0.0 g
Cholesterol 40 mg
Sodium 520 mg
Potassium 2920 mg
Total Carbohydrate 59 g
Fiber 12 g
Sugars 27 g
Protein 34 g
Phosphorus 625 mg

WEDNESDAY NIGHT

STEAK AND PORTOBELLO SANDWICH WITH TAPENADE-TOPPED TOMATOES

SERVES: 4
SERVING SIZE: 5 ounces steak, 3/4 cup mushroom, 2-ounce whole-wheat roll, 3/4 cup tomato, 1 tablespoon tapenade
PREP TIME: 5 minutes
COOKING TIME: 15 minutes

Meaty portobello mushrooms and a warm balsamic vinegar dipping sauce make this steak sandwich dinner a real treat. Buy portobello mushrooms whole and slice them after they're cooked.

A tapenade is a thick paste made from capers, olives, oil, and vinegar. For the tomato tapenade side dish, buy a good-quality tapenade and use it to top the sliced tomatoes.

HELPFUL HINTS:

- Any type of whole-wheat, 2-ounce roll can be used.

COUNTDOWN:

- Remove cooked steak left over from Sunday night from the refrigerator.
- Make side dish.
- Sauté vegetables and assemble sandwich.

STEAK AND PORTOBELLO SANDWICH

6 cloves garlic, crushed
1 cup balsamic vinegar
Olive oil spray
1/2 pound whole portobello mushrooms (about 3 3/4 cups when sliced)
4 whole-wheat hoagie (submarine) rolls (about 2 ounces each)
1 1/4 pounds grass-fed steak (saved from Sunday night)
1/2 teaspoon salt
1/4 teaspoon freshly ground black pepper

1. Mix garlic and balsamic vinegar together in a small bowl and set aside.

2. Heat a large skillet over medium-high heat. Spray with olive oil spray. Add the mushrooms and cook 5 minutes, turning over once. Remove mushrooms to a cutting board.

3. Add the balsamic vinegar mixture to the skillet and boil 3–4 minutes to reduce by half. Divide sauce among 4 small bowls to be used for dipping the sandwich.

4. Cut open rolls, spray with olive oil spray, and toast in a toaster oven for 1 minute.

5. To serve, slice steak and mushrooms into thin strips. Arrange steak and mushrooms on bottom half of the bread. Add salt and pepper. Cover with the top slice of bread and cut sandwich in half. Serve with the dipping sauce.

TAPENADE-TOPPED TOMATOES

4 tablespoons olive tapenade
3 medium ripe tomatoes, sliced
1/4 teaspoon freshly ground black pepper

1. Place tomatoes on a plate. Sprinkle with pepper. Spoon tapenade on top and serve.

COST OF MEAL PER PERSON

$9.67

PER SERVING

CHOICES/EXCHANGES
2 starch, 3 nonstarchy vegetable, 5 lean protein, 1 fat

Total Calories 510
Total Fat 15 g
Saturated Fat 3.1 g
Monounsaturated Fat 4.8 g
Trans Fat 0.0 g
Cholesterol 95 mg
Sodium 690 mg
Potassium 1350 mg
Total Carbohydrate 46 g
Fiber 6 g
Sugars 17 g
Protein 47 g
Phosphorus 600 mg

THURSDAY NIGHT

HOT AND SPICY STIR-FRY SHRIMP AND SESAME NOODLES WITH SNOW PEAS

SERVES: 4
SERVING SIZE: 5 ounces shrimp, 1/2 cup sauce and vegetables, 3/4 cup noodles, 1 3/4 cups snow peas
PREP TIME: 15 minutes
COOKING TIME: 15 minutes

Stir-fry some shrimp with hot pepper sauce, garlic, and ginger for a succulent, quick dinner. Sesame noodles with snow peas complete the meal. Fresh snow peas add a crisp texture to the noodles.

I suggest buying a bag of frozen, wild-caught shrimp to keep on hand. Look for sales and keep some in your freezer for fast, healthy meals. It saves time and money if you don't have to run to the store.

The secret to stir-fry cooking is to prepare all the ingredients first and line them up on a plate or cutting board in order of use. That way you don't have to keep looking at the recipe to know what goes in next. Another tip is to make sure your wok or skillet is very hot before adding ingredients. The oil should be smoking.

HELPFUL HINTS:

- Use a food processor to chop the onion and peanuts.
- If using ground ginger instead of fresh, mix it in with sauce.
- To save cleaning time, cook the shrimp, remove to a plate and use the same wok, without washing it, for the noodles.

COUNTDOWN:

- Stir-fry shrimp dish.
- Stir-fry noodles.

HOT AND SPICY STIR-FRY SHRIMP

1/2 cup tomato paste
1 teaspoon hot pepper sauce
1 cup water
2 teaspoons sugar
2 teaspoons sesame oil
1 cup chopped onion
4 cloves garlic, crushed
1/4 cup chopped fresh ginger
OR 4 teaspoons ground ginger
1 1/2 pounds frozen, shelled large shrimp, defrosted
2 tablespoons grated lemon rind, pith removed
4 tablespoons dry-roasted, unsalted peanuts, chopped

1. Mix tomato paste, hot pepper sauce, water, and sugar together in a bowl and set aside.

2. Heat the sesame oil in a wok or large skillet over high heat until smoking. Add the onion, garlic, and ginger and stir-fry 2 minutes. Add the shrimp and stir-fry 2–3 minutes, until the shrimp just turn pink.

3. Add tomato paste mixture and mix a few seconds. Sprinkle lemon rind into sauce. Remove to a plate and sprinkle with peanuts.

SESAME NOODLES WITH SNOW PEAS

8 ounces Chinese noodles
2 teaspoons sesame oil
1 pound snow peas (about 7 cups)
2 tablespoons sesame seeds
1/2 teaspoon salt
1/4 teaspoon freshly ground black pepper

1. Fill a large saucepan with water and bring to a boil. Add noodles, cook 1 minute and drain. Toss noodles with sesame oil.

2. Using the same wok used for the shrimp, add snow peas and stir-fry 1 minute. Add noodles and toss 2 minutes. Add sesame seeds, salt, and pepper.

3. Remove to dinner plates and serve with the shrimp on top.

COST OF MEAL PER PERSON

$8.45

PER SERVING

CHOICES/EXCHANGES
2 1/2 starch, 3 nonstarchy vegetable, 5 lean protein, 1/2 fat

Total Calories 520
Total Fat 13 g
Saturated Fat 2.2 g
Monounsaturated Fat 5.0 g
Trans Fat 0.0 g
Cholesterol 325 mg
Sodium 510 mg
Potassium 920 mg
Total Carbohydrate 53 g
Fiber 6 g
Sugars 6 g
Protein 49 g
Phosphorus 625 mg

FRIDAY NIGHT

WALNUT AND FENNEL PASTA

SERVES: 4
SERVING SIZE: 1 1/4 cups vegetables, 1/4 cup walnuts, 3/4 cup spaghetti
PREP TIME: 15 minutes
COOKING TIME: 15 minutes

This light vegetable dish features toasted walnuts and fennel. Fennel gives this dish an anise or licorice flavor. Fennel is a large white bulb with celery-like stems and green, feathery leaves. The leaves and fennel seeds add another layer of flavor to the dish. Toasting the walnuts intensifies the walnut flavor.

HELPFUL HINTS:

- Any type of whole-wheat pasta can be used.
- Walnuts can be toasted in a toaster oven or under the broiler.
- Snip the fennel leaves from the fennel stems with a scissors.

COUNTDOWN:

- Place water for pasta on to boil.
- Prepare ingredients.
- Cook pasta.
- Complete recipe.

WALNUT AND FENNEL PASTA

1 cup walnuts
6 teaspoons olive oil, divided
1 1/2 cups cubed fennel
1 1/2 cups diced onion
4 cloves garlic, crushed
2 tablespoons fennel seeds
2 cups canned, low-sodium diced tomatoes*
1/2 pound whole-wheat spaghetti
1/2 teaspoon salt
1/4 teaspoon freshly ground black pepper
1/4 cup chopped fennel leaves

1. Place a large saucepan with 3–4 quarts water on to boil for the spaghetti.

2. Coarsely chop walnuts and toast them for 1–2 minutes. Watch to make sure they do not burn.

3. Heat 2 teaspoons olive oil in a large nonstick skillet over medium-high heat. Add the fennel and onion. Sauté while stirring for 5 minutes or until onion turns golden. Add the garlic and fennel seeds and sauté another 3–4 minutes. Add the diced tomatoes and continue to cook 2–3 minutes.

4. Meanwhile, as soon as the water comes to a rolling boil, add the spaghetti and cook 8–9 minutes. Drain and add to the skillet.

5. Add the remaining 4 teaspoons olive oil and salt and pepper to the skillet. Toss well. Sprinkle walnuts and fennel leaves on top. Divide among 4 plates and serve.

**Low-sodium diced tomatoes containing per cup: 41 calories, 9.6 g carbohydrate, 24 mg sodium.*

COST OF MEAL
PER PERSON
$2.88

PER SERVING

CHOICES/EXCHANGES
2 1/2 starch,
5 nonstarchy vegetable,
5 fat

Total Calories 530
Total Fat 27 g
Saturated Fat 2.3 g
Monounsaturated fat 8.5 g
Trans Fat 0.0 g
Cholesterol 0 mg
Sodium 330 mg
Potassium 690 mg
Total Carbohydrate 61 g
Fiber 10 g
Sugars 8 g
Protein 18 g
Phosphorus 325 mg

SATURDAY NIGHT

TURKEY PESTO WRAP WITH PARMESAN CAULIFLOWER

SERVES: 4

SERVING SIZE: 5 ounces turkey, 4 teaspoons mayonnaise pesto dressing, 1 whole-wheat tortilla, 1 1/2 cups cauliflower, 1 tablespoon bread crumbs, 1 1/2 tablespoons cheese

PREP TIME: 10 minutes

COOKING TIME: 15 minutes

Turkey slices, pesto sauce, and spicy watercress rolled together in a tasty tortilla make a quick Saturday night dinner. Roasted Parmesan cauliflower completes the meal.

HELPFUL HINTS:

- Wraps can be made several hours ahead of time and refrigerated. Wrap them in plastic wrap or foil to keep them from drying out.

COUNTDOWN:

- Start cauliflower.
- While cauliflower cooks, make wraps.
- Finish cauliflower.

TURKEY PESTO WRAP

4 tablespoons reduced-fat pesto sauce
1 1/2 tablespoons reduced-fat mayonnaise
4 (8-inch) whole-wheat tortillas
1 1/4 pounds sliced, no-salt-added deli turkey breast
1 cup watercress leaves

1. Mix pesto sauce and mayonnaise together. Place tortillas on a countertop and spread with pesto mixture.

2. Arrange turkey slices on top of the pesto mixture. Divide the watercress leaves among the tortillas.

3. Roll wraps, slice in half, and serve.

Mussels in Garlic Tomato Broth p. 26–27

Mustard-Crusted Snapper with Tomato and Mint Barley p. 118–119

Mexican Fiesta Bowl p. 180–181

Five-Spice Chicken with Chinese Noodles p. 74–75

Balsamic Pork Scaloppini with Garlic Sweet Potatoes and Sugar Snap Peas p. 152–153

Lasagna Soup with Spinach Salad p. 124–125

Buffalo Chicken Legs with Blue Cheese Salad p. 172–173

Hot Glazed Pork Chops with Arugula and Walnut Salad p. 80–81

PARMESAN CAULIFLOWER

1 pound cauliflower florets (about 6 cups)
2 teaspoons olive oil
1/4 teaspoon freshly ground black pepper
1/4 cup whole-wheat bread crumbs
6 tablespoons freshly grated Parmesan cheese

1. Place cauliflower in a microwave-safe bowl and microwave on high 8 minutes or until soft.

2. Remove from microwave and toss with olive oil, pepper, bread crumbs, and Parmesan cheese. Divide among 4 dinner plates and serve with the wraps.

COST OF MEAL PER PERSON

$6.22

PER SERVING

CHOICES/EXCHANGES
2 starch, 2 nonstarchy vegetable, 5 lean protein, 1 fat

Total Calories 460
Total Fat 15 g
Saturated Fat 3.7 g
Monounsaturated Fat 4.4 g
Trans Fat 0.0 g
Cholesterol 80 mg
Sodium 670 mg
Potassium 920 mg
Total Carbohydrate 37 g
Fiber 7 g
Sugars 12 g
Protein 47 g
Phosphorus 475 mg

WEEK **SEVEN**

WEEKLY BUDGET
Average cost of a meal per person for the week is

$5.59

SUNDAY NIGHT

TURKEY AND APPLE SAUTÉ WITH SWEET POTATOES AND BROCCOLI

Sautéed turkey tenderloin is coated with an apple-flavored sauce and crisp apples and leeks. Colorful sweet potatoes and broccoli round out this delicious dinner.

MONDAY NIGHT

MUSTARD-CRUSTED SNAPPER WITH TOMATO AND MINT BARLEY

Bake this fresh snapper fillet in a tangy mustard coating that seals in the juices and adds great flavor. Savor the fresh flavors of mint and tomatoes in the 10-minute barley side dish.

TUESDAY NIGHT

TERIYAKI TURKEY WITH QUICK CASHEW RICE

Turkey tenderloin is stir-fried with red bell pepper and crunchy bok choy and tossed with sweet teriyaki sauce for an easy Chinese dinner. Finish this quick meal with microwaved brown rice mixed with cashews.

WEDNESDAY NIGHT

SNAPPER FISH SANDWICH

The bread for this tasty sandwich is spread with a mayonnaise and Old Bay seasoning mixture. Fresh snapper fillets with a crunchy cracker-crumb coating fill the sandwich for a tasty midweek supper.

THURSDAY NIGHT

LASAGNA SOUP WITH SPINACH SALAD

Try this new popular variation on lasagna. Orange zest adds an intriguing flavor to this thick soup.

FRIDAY NIGHT

VEGETABLE LO MEIN

This is a simple noodle and veggie dish made with Chinese noodles and flavored with aromatic five-spice powder. Start your weekend off right with this fun dish!

SATURDAY NIGHT

MEAT LOAF WITH MASHED SWEET POTATOES

Your family will love this comforting meat loaf. It bakes in only 15 minutes and is topped with pasta sauce. Mashed sweet potatoes complete the meal.

SHOPPING LIST

SHOP SMART

- Look for low-sodium diced tomatoes containing per cup: 41 calories, 9.6 g carbohydrate, 24 mg sodium.
- Look for low-sodium pasta sauce, containing per 1/2 cup: 112 calories, 3.5 g fat, 177.7 g carbohydrate, 39 mg sodium.
- Look for reduced-sodium teriyaki sauce, containing per tablespoon: 8 calories, 1.5 g carbohydrate, 168 mg sodium.
- Look for reduced-fat oil and vinegar dressing containing per tablespoon: 11 calories, 1.0 g fat, 4 mg sodium.

Here is the Shopping List for this week's dinners.

This shopping list will help you get in and out of the market quickly. The ingredients are listed by supermarket department to make shopping easier; you won't forget something in one department and have to go back and forth across the store.

The amount needed of each ingredient is listed so you will know what size package or can to buy. If it helps you to better visualize the amount you need, please note that 4 tablespoons equal 1/4 cup and 8 tablespoons equal 1/2 cup.

Make sure to check your refrigerator and pantry to see if you have any of these ingredients on hand before making your trip to the market.

MEAT AND SEAFOOD

3 pounds turkey tenderloin
3 pounds snapper fillets
2 pounds 95% lean ground beef

DAIRY AND EGGS

1 carton plain, nonfat Greek yogurt (1 cup needed)
Large eggs (3 needed)

BREAD AND BREAD CRUMBS

1 small package cracker meal (1/2 cup needed)
1 package whole-wheat plain bread crumbs (4 tablespoons needed)
1 package whole-wheat bread (8 slices needed)

CANNED FOODS

1 can low-sodium diced tomatoes (2 cups needed) (see *Shop Smart*, at left)
1 container fat-free, no-salt-added chicken broth (4 1/2 cups needed)
1 can low-sodium pasta sauce (2 cups needed) (see *Shop Smart*, at left)

CONDIMENTS
1 small bottle Dijon mustard (4 tablespoons needed)
1 small bottle grainy mustard (2 tablespoons needed)
1 bottle reduced-sodium teriyaki sauce (9 tablespoons needed) (see *Shop Smart*, opposite)
1 bottle reduced-fat mayonnaise (3/4 cup needed)
1 bottle oyster sauce (2 tablespoons needed)
1 bottle sesame oil (8 teaspoons needed)
1 small bottle reduced-sodium soy sauce (2 tablespoons needed)
1 bottle balsamic vinegar (1 tablespoon needed)

PASTA, RICE, AND GRAINS
1 package pearl barley (3/4 cup needed)
1 package microwaveable brown rice (to make 3 cups cooked rice)
1 package whole-wheat lasagna noodles (6 ounces needed)
1 package Chinese noodles, fresh or dried (1/2 pound needed)

SPICES
1 small bottle ground cumin (4 teaspoons needed)
1 container reduced-sodium Old Bay seasoning (2 teaspoons needed)
1 small bottle cayenne pepper (1 teaspoon needed)
1 small bottle five-spice powder (2 teaspoons needed)
1 small package fennel seeds (4 teaspoons needed)

JAM AND HONEY
1 small bottle honey (2 tablespoons needed)

NUTS
1 small package unsalted cashew nuts (1/2 cup needed)
1 small package walnuts (4 tablespoons needed)

FROZEN FOODS
1 package frozen diced or chopped onion (2 cups needed)

JUICE AND WINE
1 small bottle apple juice (1 cup needed)
1 small bottle dry sherry (4 tablespoons needed)

PRODUCE
2 Granny Smith apples (2 cups needed)
5 medium onions (5 1/2 cups needed)
1 red onion (1 1/2 cups needed)
1 package shredded carrots (1 cup needed)
2 red bell peppers (2 cups needed)
1 bok choy (4 cups sliced needed)
1 head romaine lettuce (several leaves needed)
1 package washed, ready-to-eat spinach (6 cups needed)
1 package snow peas (1 1/2 cups needed)
2 tomatoes (3 cups needed)
1 package sliced mushrooms (3 1/2 cups needed)
1 large leek (1 1/2 cups needed)
1 bunch celery (2 cups sliced needed)
1 bunch basil (1 cup needed)
1 bunch fresh mint (4 tablespoons needed)
1 piece fresh ginger (1 1/2 tablespoons needed)
1 package bean sprouts (1 1/2 cups needed)
1 bunch scallions (1 1/2 cups sliced needed)
1 lemon (1 tablespoon needed)
1 orange
3 pounds sweet potatoes
1/2 pound broccoli florets

STAPLES
Olive oil spray
Olive oil
Canola oil
Garlic (20 cloves needed)
Reduced-fat oil and vinegar dressing (see *Shop Smart*, opposite)
Cornstarch
Salt
Black peppercorns

SUNDAY NIGHT

TURKEY AND APPLE SAUTÉ WITH SWEET POTATOES AND BROCCOLI

SERVES: 4
SERVING SIZE: 5 ounces turkey breast, 1/2 cup apples, 1/2 cup leeks, 1/4 cup sauce, 1 1/4 cups sweet potato, 3/4 cup broccoli, 1 teaspoon olive oil
PREP TIME: 20 minutes
COOKING TIME: 20 minutes

Crisp, juicy apples add flavor and texture to this dinner. Apples should be stored in the refrigerator and, if washed, dried thoroughly before refrigerating. This recipe calls for Granny Smith apples, which are green, tart, juicy, and crisp; this type of apple creates a pleasing contrast with the turkey.

Turkey can be found in a variety of cuts in the markets. Turkey tenderloins are the heart of the breast meat. They are the same shape as veal or beef tenderloins. If you use a thinner cut of turkey such as a turkey steak or cutlet, reduce the cooking time by half. Half the turkey is used for this dinner. The remaining half is used for Tuesday night's dinner.

Sweet potatoes that are boiled and tossed with olive oil and broccoli florets make an attractive and delicious side dish.

HELPFUL HINTS:

- Leeks look like a giant scallion with broad, dark green leaves that are tightly wrapped around each other. The quickest way to clean them is to trim the root end and make 4 to 5 slits from top to bottom. Run the leaves under cold water to reach the dirt trapped between the leaf layers.

COUNTDOWN:

- Place potatoes on to boil.
- Prepare turkey.
- Complete potatoes and broccoli.

TURKEY AND APPLE SAUTÉ

1 1/2 pounds turkey tenderloin
Olive oil spray
1/2 teaspoon salt
1/4 teaspoon freshly ground black pepper
1 1/2 cups washed and sliced leeks
2 Granny Smith apples, cored, sliced, and cut into quarters (2 cups)
1 cup water, divided
2 teaspoons cornstarch
1 cup apple juice

1. Cut turkey tenderloin into 1-inch slices. Heat a large nonstick skillet over medium-high heat and spray with olive oil spray. Add the turkey and brown 5 minutes, turning to make sure all sides are browned. A meat thermometer inserted into turkey should read 170°F. Remove to a plate. Sprinkle with salt and pepper.

2. Lower heat under the skillet and add leeks and apples. Sauté for 5 minutes without browning, turning them with a fork to prevent breaking.

3. In a small bowl, mix 2 tablespoons of the water with the cornstarch until smooth and set aside.

4. Add the apple juice and remaining water to the pan, scraping up any brown bits in the bottom of the skillet. Add the cornstarch mixture and simmer until the sauce thickens, about 1 minute. Return turkey slices to the skillet for a minute to warm through.

5. Divide turkey among 4 plates. Spoon apples, leeks, and sauce on top of turkey slices.

SWEET POTATOES AND BROCCOLI

1 1/2 pounds sweet potatoes, peeled and sliced 1/4–1/2 inch thick
1/2 pound broccoli florets
4 teaspoons olive oil
1/4 teaspoon salt
1/4 teaspoon freshly ground black

1. Place sliced potatoes in a large saucepan. Add cold water to cover. Cover pan with a lid and bring to a boil. Cook 1 minute.

2. Add the broccoli florets and continue to boil, uncovered, 5 minutes or until potatoes are soft.

3. Drain and toss vegetables with the oil, salt, and pepper. Divide into 4 portions and place on plates with the turkey.

COST OF MEAL PER PERSON

$4.15

PER SERVING

CHOICES/EXCHANGES
2 starch, 1 fruit,
2 nonstarchy vegetable,
5 lean protein

Total Calories 500
Total Fat 11 g
Saturated Fat 1.5 g
Monounsaturated Fat 4.0 g
Trans Fat 0.0 g
Cholesterol 90 mg
Sodium 680 mg
Potassium 1345 mg
Total Carbohydrate 60 g
Fiber 8 g
Sugars 21 g
Protein 45 g
Phosphorus 450 mg

MONDAY NIGHT

MUSTARD-CRUSTED SNAPPER WITH TOMATO AND MINT BARLEY

SERVES: 4
SERVING SIZE: 5 ounces snapper, 2 tablespoons honey mustard sauce, 1/2 cup barley, 1 cup vegetables
PREP TIME: 10 minutes
COOKING TIME: 25 minutes

A tangy mustard coating gives this baked fish great flavor and seals in the juices. I use two types of mustard in this recipe—Dijon and a grainy mustard. This recipe is very simple and, once it is in the oven, you can quickly make the barley. Half the snapper is used for this dinner. The remaining half is used for Wednesday night's dinner.

Barley is a grain used most often in stews and soups, but it is very good boiled and served as an alternative to rice. It adds a crunchy texture to the meal. Look for quick-cooking barley, which cooks in half the time of regular barley. Otherwise, regular barley can be used; it cooks in about 30 minutes.

HELPFUL HINTS:

- Any type of fish fillet such as sole or tilapia can be used in this recipe. Adjust the cooking time according to the thickness of fish. A 1 1/2-inch fillet takes 20 minutes to bake in a preheated oven.
- Brown rice can be substituted for barley if you prefer.

COUNTDOWN:

- Preheat oven to 400°F.
- Prepare fish and place in oven.
- Make barley.

MUSTARD-CRUSTED SNAPPER

Olive oil spray
4 tablespoons Dijon mustard
2 tablespoons grainy mustard
4 teaspoons ground cumin
2 tablespoons honey
1 1/2 pounds snapper fillets
1/4 teaspoon freshly ground black pepper

1. Preheat oven to 400°F. Line a baking tray with foil and lightly spray with olive oil spray.

2. In a small bowl, stir together the mustards, cumin, and honey. Rinse fish and pat dry. Spoon mustard coating on both sides of fish and place on prepared baking tray.

3. For fish fillets 1 1/2 inches thick, bake 20 minutes. Place fish on individual plates and pour pan juices over the top. Sprinkle with pepper.

TOMATO AND MINT BARLEY

3 cups water
3/4 cup quick-cooking pearl barley
2 tablespoons olive oil, divided
2 cups diced onion
2 cups diced tomato
4 tablespoons chopped fresh mint
1/2 teaspoon salt
1/4 teaspoon freshly ground black pepper

1. Bring water to a boil and stir in barley. When water returns to a boil, reduce the heat to medium, cover, and simmer 10 minutes. Drain and set aside.

2. Heat 1 teaspoon oil in a nonstick skillet and sauté onion until transparent and golden, about 10 minutes. Add tomatoes and sauté 2 minutes.

3. Add barley, mint, and remaining oil. Toss well. Add salt and pepper and serve.

COST OF MEAL
PER PERSON
$9.51

PER SERVING

CHOICES/EXCHANGES
2 starch, 1 carbohydrate,
2 nonstarchy vegetable,
4 lean protein, 1 fat

Total Calories 490
Total Fat 13 g
Saturated Fat 1.9 g
Monounsaturated Fat 5.9 g
Trans Fat 0.0 g
Cholesterol 60 mg
Sodium 670 mg
Potassium 1265 mg
Total Carbohydrate 53 g
Fiber 11 g
Sugars 16 g
Protein 42 g
Phosphorus 500 mg

TUESDAY NIGHT

TERIYAKI TURKEY WITH QUICK CASHEW RICE

SERVES: 4
SERVING SIZE: 5 ounces turkey breast, 2 cups vegetables, 2 1/4 tablespoons sauce, 3/4 cup brown rice, 2 tablespoons cashew nuts
PREP TIME: 10 minutes
COOKING TIME: 15 minutes

Stir-fried crunchy vegetables and turkey in a sweet teriyaki sauce make a colorful, quick dinner. This dinner only takes minutes to prepare using bottled teriyaki sauce.

Here are a few wok-cooking tips: Make sure your wok is very hot before adding the ingredients. The oil should be smoking. For easy stir-frying, place all of the prepared ingredients on a cutting board or plate in order of use. That way you won't have to keep looking at the recipe once you start to cook. If you don't have a large enough wok or skillet to hold all of the ingredients, divide the ingredients in half and cook each half separately.

HELPFUL HINTS:

- Napa or Chinese cabbage can be substituted for the bok choy.
- Green pepper can be substituted for red pepper.

COUNTDOWN:

- Prepare all ingredients.
- Make rice and set aside.
- Stir-fry turkey dish.

TERIYAKI TURKEY

2 teaspoons cornstarch
2 tablespoons water
2 teaspoons canola oil
1 1/2 cups sliced red onion
2 cups sliced red bell pepper
4 cups sliced bok choy
6 cloves garlic, crushed
1 1/2 pounds turkey tenderloin, cut into 1/2-inch strips
9 tablespoons bottled reduced-sodium teriyaki sauce*

1. Mix cornstarch with water in a small bowl and set aside.

2. Heat canola oil in a wok or skillet over high heat. When oil is smoking, add the onion, red pepper, bok choy, and garlic. Stir-fry 5 minutes.

3. Add the turkey to the wok and stir-fry 3 minutes.

4. Move ingredients to the sides of the wok, leaving a hole in the center. Add the teriyaki sauce and cornstarch mixture. Toss the ingredients with the sauce for about 1 minute or until the sauce starts to thicken and coats the food. Serve over rice.

**Look for reduced-sodium teriyaki sauce, containing per tablespoon: 8 calories, 1.5 g carbohydrate, 168 mg sodium.*

QUICK CASHEW RICE

Microwaveable brown rice (to make 3 cups cooked rice)
2 teaspoons canola oil
1/2 cup unsalted cashew nuts
1/4 teaspoon freshly ground black pepper

1. Cook rice according to package instructions.

2. Measure 3 cups into a bowl and reserve any remaining rice for another meal. Add the oil, cashews, and pepper to the rice. Toss well.

COST OF MEAL PER PERSON

$5.11

PER SERVING

CHOICES/EXCHANGES
2 starch, 1/2 carbohydrate, 4 nonstarchy vegetable, 5 lean protein, 1 1/2 fat

Total Calories 590
Total Fat 18 g
Saturated Fat 2.9 g
Monounsaturated Fat 8.5 g
Trans Fat 0.0 g
Cholesterol 90 mg
Sodium 670 mg
Potassium 940 mg
Total Carbohydrate 60 g
Fiber 6 g
Sugars 10 g
Protein 50 g
Phosphorus 525 mg

WEDNESDAY NIGHT

SNAPPER FISH SANDWICH

SERVES: 4

SERVING SIZE: 5 ounces snapper, 2 slices whole-wheat bread, 1/2 cup vegetables, 3 tablespoons mayonnaise dressing

PREP TIME: 15 minutes

COOKING TIME: 15 minutes

Here's a quick sandwich supper. It's a perfect midweek meal that's easy to make.

HELPFUL HINTS:

- Any type of fish fillet such as sole or tilapia can be used instead of snapper.

COUNTDOWN:

- Prepare ingredients.
- Mix mayonnaise sauce.
- Cook fish and complete the recipe.

SNAPPER FISH SANDWICH

3/4 cup reduced-fat mayonnaise
1 tablespoon lemon juice
2 teaspoons reduced-sodium Old Bay seasoning
2 egg whites
1/2 cup cracker meal
1 1/2 pounds snapper fillets
2 teaspoons canola oil
1/4 teaspoon freshly ground black pepper
8 slices whole-wheat bread
Several lettuce leaves
1 tomato, sliced

1. Mix mayonnaise, lemon juice, and Old Bay seasoning together in a small bowl and set aside.

2. Add egg whites to a bowl and lightly beat them with a fork. Place cracker crumbs on a plate. Dip the fish fillets into the egg whites then into the cracker meal. Press the meal into the fish on both sides.

3. Heat oil in a large nonstick skillet over medium-high heat. Add the fish in one layer and sauté for 1 minute, turn, and sauté on second side for 1 minute. Reduce heat to low and continue to cook 3 minutes for a 1/2-inch-thick fillet. Sprinkle pepper over the fish.

4. Toast bread. Divide fish among 4 bread slices. Place lettuce and sliced tomato over the fish. Spread the mayonnaise mixture over the remaining bread slices and close sandwiches with them. Cut in half and serve.

COST OF MEAL
PER PERSON

$8.56

PER SERVING

CHOICES/EXCHANGES
2 1/2 starch, 1 nonstarchy vegetable, 5 lean protein, 2 1/2 fat

Total Calories 560
Total Fat 22 g
Saturated Fat 3.3 g
Monounsaturated Fat 5.7 g
Trans Fat 0.0 g
Cholesterol 60 mg
Sodium 610mg
Potassium 1085 mg
Total Carbohydrate 42 g
Fiber 5 g
Sugars 6 g
Protein 43 g
Phosphorus 505 mg

THURSDAY NIGHT

LASAGNA SOUP WITH SPINACH SALAD

SERVES: 4
SERVING SIZE: 3 ounces ground beef, 1 1/2 cups vegetables, 1/2 cup lasagna, 1 1/2 cups soup, 1/4 cup yogurt, 1 1/2 cups spinach, 1 tablespoon walnuts, 1 tablespoon dressing
PREP TIME: 15 minutes
COOKING TIME: 25 minutes

Everyone loves lasagna! This is a new and popular variation on lasagna that is served in bowls as a thick soup. The soup is served with dollop of yogurt for a light, creamy finish.

Orange zest adds an intriguing, sweet flavor to this soup. The zest is created by scraping or cutting the outer skin of an unwaxed orange. Be sure not to include the white pith, which lies just under the skin, when zesting the orange.

HELPFUL HINTS:

- Pecan halves or other nuts can be used instead of walnuts in the salad.

COUNTDOWN:

- Prepare all ingredients.
- Start soup.
- While soup cooks, toast walnuts and make salad.

LASAGNA SOUP

2 tablespoons canola oil
2 cups diced onion
1 cup shredded carrots
6 cloves garlic, crushed
1 pound 95% lean ground beef
1/2 teaspoon salt
1/4 teaspoon freshly ground black pepper
4 cups fat-free, no-salt-added chicken broth
2 cups canned, low-sodium diced tomatoes with the liquid*
Zest of 1 orange
6 ounces whole-wheat lasagna noodles, broken into 1–2-inch pieces
1 cup fresh basil leaves
1 cup plain, nonfat Greek yogurt

1. Heat canola oil in a large saucepan and add the onion and carrots. Sauté 5 minutes, then add the garlic and sauté for 1 minute.

2. Add the ground beef. Brown the meat 3–4 minutes and season with salt and pepper.

3. Stir in the chicken broth, diced tomatoes, and orange zest. Bring to a boil and add the noodles. Lower the heat and simmer 10 minutes or until the noodles are soft.

4. Stir in the basil. Serve in soup bowls and add a dollop yogurt on top of each serving.

**Look for low-sodium diced tomatoes containing per cup: 41 calories, 9.6 g carbohydrate, 24 mg sodium.*

SPINACH SALAD

4 tablespoons walnut halves
6 cups washed, ready-to-eat spinach
4 tablespoons reduced-fat oil and vinegar dressing**

1. Place walnuts in a toaster oven for 1 minute to toast, or warm them in a small skillet without oil for 1 minute. Watch them, they will burn easily.

2. Add spinach to a bowl and toss with the salad dressing. Sprinkle toasted walnuts on top.

***Look for reduced-fat oil and vinegar dressing containing per tablespoon: 11 calories, 1.0 g fat, 4 mg sodium.*

COST OF MEAL PER PERSON

$4.71

PER SERVING

CHOICES/EXCHANGES
1 1/2 starch, 1 carbohydrate, 3 nonstarchy vegetable, 4 lean protein, 2 fat

Total Calories 550
Total Fat 19 g
Saturated Fat 3.7 g
Monounsaturated Fat 8.3 g
Trans Fat 0.0 g
Cholesterol 75 mg
Sodium 630 mg
Potassium 1745 mg
Total Carbohydrate 56 g
Fiber 10 g
Sugars 14 g
Protein 43 g
Phosphorus 690 mg

FRIDAY NIGHT

VEGETABLE LO MEIN

SERVES: 4

SERVING SIZE: 3/4 cup noodles, 2 1/4 cups vegetables, 5 tablespoons sauce

PREP TIME: 15 minutes

COOKING TIME: 15 minutes

Stir up a colorful noodle-veggie meal in a flash! This quick Chinese meal will rival your local restaurant favorites. I have used only vegetables in this dish, which I chose for their variety of flavors, colors, and textures. The vegetables are added to the wok and removed in stages so that the wok will not become overcrowded.

Five-spice powder is an aromatic mixture of five ground spices, usually consisting of cinnamon, cloves, fennel seed, star anise, and Szechuan peppercorns. It makes a flavorful addition to the recipe, and can also be used when cooking rice or other vegetables.

HELPFUL HINTS:

- Make sure your wok or skillet is very hot before you start to cook.
- Arrange all of the ingredients on a chopping board or plate in order of cooking, so you won't have to refer to the recipe as you cook.

COUNTDOWN:

- Place a pot of water for noodles on to boil.
- Mix sauce ingredients together.
- Wash and cut vegetables.
- Cook noodles.
- Stir-fry vegetables and noodles.

VEGETABLE LO MEIN

1/2 pound dried or fresh Chinese noodles
1/2 cup fat free, no-salt-added chicken broth
4 tablespoons dry sherry
2 tablespoons oyster sauce
2 tablespoons reduced-sodium soy sauce
1 tablespoon cornstarch
1 teaspoon cayenne pepper
2 teaspoons ground five-spice powder
8 teaspoons sesame oil, divided
1 1/2 cups sliced onion
2 cups sliced celery
6 cloves garlic, crushed
1 1/2 tablespoons chopped fresh ginger
1 1/2 cups fresh snow peas
1 1/2 cups fresh bean sprouts
3 cups sliced mushrooms

1. Fill a large saucepan with water, bring it to a boil, and add noodles. Boil 2–3 minutes and drain.

2. While water comes to a boil, prepare sauce and vegetables: mix chicken broth, sherry, oyster sauce, soy sauce, cornstarch, cayenne pepper, and five-spice powder together and set aside.

3. Heat 2 teaspoons sesame oil in a wok or large skillet over high heat until smoking. Add onion and celery. Stir-fry 3 minutes. Remove to a bowl. Add garlic, ginger, snow peas, bean sprouts, and mushrooms to the wok. Toss 4 minutes. Remove to bowl with the onion and celery.

4. Add the remaining 6 teaspoons sesame oil to the skillet. When it starts to smoke, add the drained noodles. Stir-fry 2–3 minutes, stirring constantly.

5. Return the vegetables to the wok. Move the ingredients to the sides of the wok leaving a hole in the center. Add sauce and toss 3 more minutes making sure the sauce coats the ingredients.

COST OF MEAL PER PERSON
$3.46

PER SERVING

CHOICES/EXCHANGES
2 starch, 1 carbohydrate,
3 nonstarchy vegetable, 2 fat

Total Calories 410
Total Fat 12 g
Saturated Fat 2.1 g
Monounsaturated Fat 4.5 g
Trans Fat 0.0 g
Cholesterol 50 mg
Sodium 590 mg
Potassium 735 mg
Total Carbohydrate 60 g
Fiber 6 g
Sugars 8 g
Protein 14 g
Phosphorus 285 mg

SATURDAY NIGHT

MEAT LOAF WITH MASHED SWEET POTATOES

SERVES: 4
SERVING SIZE: 3 ounces ground beef, 1/2 cup onion, 1 tablespoon bread crumbs, 2 tablespoons mushrooms, 1/2 cup pasta sauce, 1 1/4 cups potatoes, 6 tablespoons scallions, 1 1/2 teaspoons oil
PREP TIME: 15 minutes
COOKING TIME: 20 minutes

Meat loaf, well seasoned and served with a tomato-mushroom sauce, makes a delicious entree. The meat loaves for this recipe bake on a baking sheet instead of in a loaf pan. The hot air circulates around the loaves and they bake faster this way.

HELPFUL HINTS:

- Ground buffalo can be used instead of lean ground beef.

COUNTDOWN:

- Preheat oven to 400°F.
- Make meat loaves.
- While meat loaves bake, make sweet potatoes.

MEAT LOAF

Olive oil spray
1 pound 95% lean ground beef
4 teaspoons fennel seeds
4 tablespoons whole-wheat plain bread crumbs
2 cups chopped or diced frozen onion
2 cloves garlic
1 tablespoon balsamic vinegar
1/2 teaspoon salt
1/4 teaspoon freshly ground black pepper
1 large egg
1/2 cup sliced mushrooms
2 cups low-sodium pasta sauce*

1. Preheat oven to 400°F. Line a baking sheet with foil and spray with olive oil spray.

2. Mix ground beef, fennel seeds, bread crumbs, onion, garlic, and balsamic vinegar together in a large bowl. Add salt, pepper, and the egg. Mix together. Shape into 4 loaves about 5 × 3 inches each and place them on the baking sheet.

3. Spread mushrooms and pasta sauce on top of the loaves. Bake 15 minutes. A meat thermometer inserted into loaves should read 160°F.

**Look for low-sodium pasta sauce, containing per 1/2 cup: 112 calories, 3.5 g fat, 177.7 g carbohydrate, 39 mg sodium.*

MASHED SWEET POTATOES

1 1/2 pounds sweet potatoes
1 1/2 cups sliced scallions
2 tablespoons canola oil
1/4 teaspoon salt
1/4 teaspoon freshly ground black pepper

1. Microwave method: Wash potatoes but do not peel. Prick skin with a knife in several places. Wrap potatoes in paper towels and microwave on high 6 minutes or until soft when tested with a knife. Cut potatoes in half lengthwise, then scoop out flesh into a bowl and coarsely mash with a fork. (Then proceed to step #3.)

2. Stove-top method: Wash, peel, and cut potatoes into 2-inch pieces. Place in a saucepan and cover with cold water. Cover saucepan with a lid and bring to a boil. Reduce heat and simmer 10 minutes. Drain potatoes and mash. (Then proceed to step #3.)

3. Add scallions to the mashed potatoes. Mix in oil, salt, and pepper. Serve with meat loaf.

COST OF MEAL
PER PERSON
$3.61

PER SERVING

CHOICES/EXCHANGES
3 1/2 starch, 1 nonstarchy vegetable, 3 lean protein, 2 1/2 fat

Total Calories 540
Total Fat 18 g
Saturated Fat 3.9 g
Monounsaturated Fat 9.0 g
Trans Fat 0.0 g
Cholesterol 120 mg
Sodium 690 mg
Potassium 1695 mg
Total Carbohydrate 61 g
Fiber 11 g
Sugars 20 g
Protein 33 g
Phosphorus 445 mg

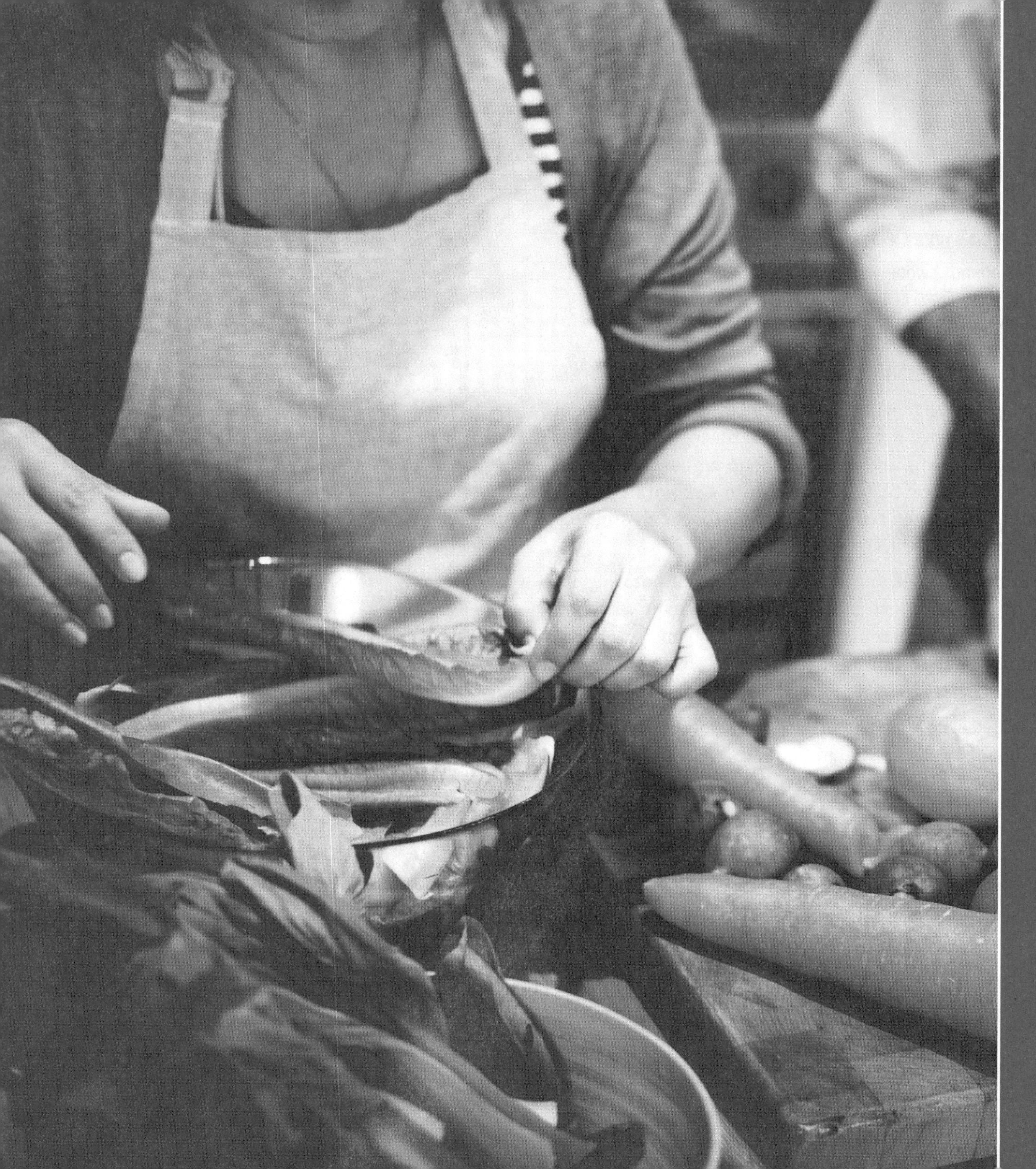

WEEK **EIGHT**

WEEKLY BUDGET
Average cost of a meal per person for the week is
$4.59

SUNDAY NIGHT
LAMB AND ASPARAGUS WITH GARLIC MINT SAUCE AND ROASTED RED POTATOES

Lamb cubes cut from the leg of lamb and asparagus are served in a sauce made with sweet mint jelly and lemon juice. The lamb and asparagus go perfectly with roasted potatoes.

MONDAY NIGHT
WASABI TUNA WITH PAN-ROASTED CORN AND LIMA BEANS

For this dinner, seared tuna steaks are topped with spicy wasabi sauce and served with corn, lima beans, and red bell pepper sautéed with fresh ginger.

TUESDAY NIGHT
TARRAGON HERBED CHICKEN WITH BROWN RICE

Flavor your chicken with a fresh herb mixture made with tarragon, parsley, and mushrooms. This delicious chicken preparation is served over brown rice.

WEDNESDAY NIGHT
TUNA SKILLET PIE

The smoky sweetness of chipotle peppers adds a special flavor to this tuna noodle pie. This is a quick meal perfect for midweek.

THURSDAY NIGHT
CHICKEN PANINI WITH ITALIAN SALAD

This panini has a warm, tasty filling of melted cheese, chicken, and fresh tarragon. Finish the meal with an Italian-style salad.

FRIDAY NIGHT
ONION, PEPPER, AND MUSHROOM PIZZA

It's pizza night! Enjoy this thin whole-wheat crust topped with Swiss cheese, mushrooms, peppers, tomatoes, and onion. It's a vegetarian meal.

SATURDAY NIGHT
SPICED LAMB STEAK WITH FLORENTINE RICE

Allspice, cinnamon, and cayenne pepper form a spice coating for lamb steaks, which are cut from the leg of lamb. Microwaved brown rice mixed with fresh spinach completes the dinner.

SHOPPING LIST

Here is the Shopping List for this week's dinners.

This shopping list will help you get in and out of the market quickly. The ingredients are listed by supermarket department to make shopping easier; you won't forget something in one department and have to go back and forth across the store.

The amount needed of each ingredient is listed so you will know what size package or can to buy. If it helps you to better visualize the amount you need, please note that 4 tablespoons equal 1/4 cup and 8 tablespoons equal 1/2 cup.

Make sure to check your refrigerator and pantry to see if you have any of these ingredients on hand before making your trip to the market.

MEAT AND SEAFOOD

1 1/2 pounds lamb cubes cut from the leg
4 (6-ounce) lamb steaks center cut from the leg
3 pounds tuna steaks
3 pounds boneless skinless chicken breasts

DAIRY

1 package shredded, reduced-fat sharp cheddar cheese (1 1/2 cups needed)
12 ounces reduced-fat Swiss cheese

BAKERY

1 loaf whole-wheat bread (8, 1-ounce slices needed)
1 (12-inch) thin-crust whole-wheat pizza base (such as Boboli brand)

SHOP SMART

- Look for low-sodium, no-sugar-added pasta sauce containing per 1 cup: 103 calories, 0.5 g fat, 21.3 g carbohydrate, 21 mg sodium.
- Look for reduced-fat oil and vinegar dressing containing per tablespoon: 11 calories, 1.0 g fat, 4 mg sodium.

CONDIMENTS

1 small jar reduced-fat mayonnaise (4 tablespoons needed)

CANNED FOODS

1 can low-sodium tomato sauce (2 cups needed) (see *Shop Smart*, opposite)
1 container fat-free, no-salt-added chicken broth (2 cups needed)

PASTA AND GRAINS

Microwaveable brown rice (to make 6 cups cooked rice)
1/2 pound fresh whole-wheat linguine

SPICES

1 small bottle cayenne pepper (1/4 teaspoon needed)
1 small bottle chipotle powder (1/4 teaspoon needed)
1 small bottle ground allspice (2 teaspoons needed)
1 small bottle ground cinnamon (2 teaspoons needed)
1 small bottle dried oregano (2 teaspoons needed)
1 small bottle wasabi powder (4 teaspoons needed)

JAM AND HONEY

1 small jar mint jelly (2 tablespoons needed)

FROZEN

1 package corn kernels (2 cups needed)
1 package lima beans (3 cups needed)

PRODUCE

1 pound thin asparagus
1 small piece fresh ginger (2 tablespoons needed)
2 lemons
1 container sliced baby bello mushrooms (6 3/4 cups needed)
2 onions (1 1/2 cups needed)
2 Vidalia or other sweet onions (2 cups needed)
2 green, yellow, or red bell peppers
4 red bell peppers (4 cups needed)
4 green bell peppers (4 cups needed)
2 pounds red potatoes
1 package washed, ready-to-eat spinach (10 cups needed)
1 bag washed, ready-to-eat Italian-style salad greens (8 cups needed)
1 package arugula (2 cups needed)
3 ripe tomatoes (3 cups needed)
1 bunch fresh tarragon (11 tablespoons chopped leaves needed)
1 bunch parsley (3/4 cup chopped leaves needed)

STAPLES

Black peppercorns
Canola oil (10 teaspoons needed)
Flour (2 tablespoons needed)
Garlic (7 cloves needed)
Olive oil spray
Olive oil
Reduced-fat oil and vinegar dressing (see *Shop Smart*, opposite)
Salt

SUNDAY NIGHT

LAMB AND ASPARAGUS WITH GARLIC MINT SAUCE AND ROASTED RED POTATOES

SERVES: 4
SERVING SIZE: 5 ounces lamb, 3/4 cup asparagus,1/3 cup sauce, 1 1/2 cups potatoes
PREP TIME: 10 minutes
COOKING TIME: 40 minutes

Lamb cubes cut from the leg are perfect for this dish. If lamb cubes are not available in your market's meat case, ask the butcher to cut some for you from a leg of lamb.

Keep in mind when shopping this week that you will need to buy 2 types of lamb cut from the leg: lamb cubes for tonight and lamb steak for Saturday night's dinner.

HELPFUL HINTS:

- Any type of red, white, or yellow waxy potato can be used.
- Try to buy the pencil-thin asparagus. If unavailable, cut thicker asparagus stalks in half lengthwise and then into 2-inch pieces.
- For quick, even roasting of the potatoes, use an ovenproof dish large enough to hold the potatoes in one layer without overlapping.

COUNTDOWN:

- Preheat oven to 425°F.
- Start potatoes.
- While potatoes bake, make lamb.

LAMB AND ASPARAGUS WITH GARLIC MINT SAUCE

Olive oil spray
1 1/2 pounds lamb cubes cut from leg (1 1/2-inch cubes)
2 tablespoons flour
6 cloves garlic, crushed
1 pound thin asparagus, washed and cut into 2-inch pieces
1 cup fat-free, no-salt-added chicken broth
2 tablespoons mint jelly
2 tablespoons lemon juice
1/4 teaspoon salt
1/4 teaspoon freshly ground black pepper

1. Heat a nonstick skillet (that is just large enough to hold lamb cubes in one layer) over medium-high heat. Spray with olive oil spray. Add lamb and brown 2 minutes. Turn and brown 2 more minutes. A meat thermometer inserted into lamb should read 125°F for rare, 145°F for medium. Remove to a plate.

2. Lower heat and add flour, garlic, and asparagus to the skillet. Toss until flour is absorbed.

3. Add chicken broth. Simmer 3 minutes, scraping up any brown bits in the bottom of the skillet. Add mint jelly and lemon juice. Stir until jelly is dissolved, about 1 minute.

4. Return lamb to the skillet and toss well. Sprinkle with salt and pepper. Serve over potatoes.

See p. 135, following photo insert, for Roasted Red Potatoes

ROASTED RED POTATOES

Olive oil spray
2 pounds red potatoes, washed, not peeled, and cut into1-inch pieces
1 cup fat-free, no-salt-added chicken broth
1/2 teaspoon salt
1/4 teaspoon freshly ground black pepper

1. Preheat oven to 425°F and spray a 9 × 13-inch pan or other large baking pan with olive oil spray.

2. Add potatoes and broth to the baking pan. Bake 40 minutes. Check after 20 minutes; if the pan is very dry, add a little water. At the end of the cooking time, liquid will be nearly evaporated and potatoes will be brown.

3. Sprinkle with salt and pepper. Serve the potatoes on individual plates and pour any remaining liquid over them.

See p. 134, preceding photo insert, for Lamb and Asparagus with Garlic Mint Sauce

COST OF MEAL PER PERSON

$4.50

PER SERVING

CHOICES/EXCHANGES
2 1/2 starch, 1/2 carbohydrate,
1 nonstarchy vegetable,
5 lean protein, 1/2 fat

Total Calories 500
Total Fat 14 g
Saturated Fat 3.6 g
Monounsaturated Fat 6.3 g
Trans Fat 0.0 g
Cholesterol 110 mg
Sodium 670 mg
Potassium 1700 mg
Total Carbohydrate 54 g
Fiber 7 g
Sugars 10 g
Protein 44 g
Phosphorus 540 mg

MONDAY NIGHT

WASABI TUNA WITH PAN-ROASTED CORN AND LIMA BEANS

SERVES: 4
SERVING SIZE: 5 ounces tuna, 1 tablespoon sauce, 1 3/4 cups vegetables
PREP TIME: 10 minutes
COOKING TIME: 10 minutes

Spicy wasabi sauce gives pan-seared fresh tuna an Asian flavor. Wasabi is the Japanese version of horseradish. It's an Asian root vegetable that is sold in paste and powdered forms. Fresh wasabi root can be found in some Asian stores as well.

I use frozen tuna steaks for this recipe. Look for wild-caught tuna that is flash frozen when it is caught. Buy 3 pounds for this week's dinners. Use 1 1/2 pounds for this recipe, and save the rest for Wednesday night's dinner.

To save time and cleanup, the tuna and vegetables are cooked in the same skillet. Make the tuna first, spread the sauce on top, and remove from the skillet. Then use the same skillet for the Pan-Roasted Corn and Lima Beans.

HELPFUL HINTS:

- Prepared horseradish can be used instead of wasabi powder, if desired.
- Ground ginger can be substituted for fresh ginger.
- A quick way to chop fresh ginger is to press it though a garlic press with large holes.
- A quick way to defrost corn and lima beans is to place them in a strainer and run hot water over them.

COUNTDOWN:

- Make tuna and sauce.
- Make corn and lima beans.

WASABI TUNA

4 tablespoons reduced-fat oil and vinegar dressing*
4 teaspoons wasabi powder
2 teaspoons canola oil
1 1/2 pounds tuna steaks
1/4 teaspoon salt
1/4 teaspoon freshly ground black pepper

**Look for reduced-fat oil and vinegar dressing containing per tablespoon: 11 calories, 1.0 g fat, 4 mg sodium.*

1. Mix the dressing with the wasabi powder in a small bowl and set aside.

2. Heat oil in a large nonstick skillet over medium-high heat. Add the tuna and sear for 2 minutes for 1 1/2-inch-thick tuna steaks. Turn and sear the other side for 1 minute. Sprinkle tuna with salt and pepper.

3. Remove skillet from heat and place tuna on a plate. Spread the wasabi sauce over the tuna. Cover with another plate or foil to keep warm until the vegetables are ready. Use the same skillet for the side dish.

PAN-ROASTED CORN AND LIMA BEANS

4 teaspoons canola oil
2 tablespoons chopped fresh ginger or 4 teaspoons ground ginger
2 cups frozen corn kernels, defrosted
3 cups frozen lima beans, defrosted
2 cups sliced red bell peppers, sliced
1/2 teaspoon salt
1/4 teaspoon freshly ground black pepper

1. Add the oil to the nonstick skillet used for the tuna and heat over medium-high heat.

2. Add the ginger, corn, lima beans, and red peppers. Toss to coat the vegetables with the oil and cover with a lid. Cook 5 minutes.

3. Sprinkle with salt and pepper and serve with the tuna.

COST OF MEAL PER PERSON

$4.83

PER SERVING

CHOICES/EXCHANGES
3 starch, 1 nonstarchy vegetable, 6 lean protein

Total Calories 510
Total Fat 10 g
Saturated Fat 1.2 g
Monounsaturated Fat 5.1 g
Trans Fat 0.0 g
Cholesterol 80 mg
Sodium 570 mg
Potassium 825 mg
Total Carbohydrate 50 g
Fiber 10 g
Sugars 6 g
Protein 52 g
Phosphorus 190 mg

TUESDAY NIGHT

TARRAGON HERBED CHICKEN WITH BROWN RICE

SERVES: 4

SERVING SIZE: 5 ounces chicken, 1/3 cup herbs and mushrooms, 3/4 cup rice, 1 cup vegetables, 1 teaspoon oil

PREP TIME: 10 minutes

COOKING TIME: 10 minutes

Boneless, skinless chicken breast cutlets are used for both this dinner and Thursday's Chicken Panini. Cook the chicken for both nights when making this recipe and then save half for Thursday's quick supper. You will need to use two skillets to fit all of the chicken.

Fresh tarragon gives a fragrant anise or licorice flavor to the chicken. If you prefer, you can use basil, cilantro, or dill instead.

HELPFUL HINTS:

- Dried tarragon can be used instead of fresh. Use 1 teaspoon dried.
- Look for microwaveable brown rice, enough to make 3 cups cooked rice.

COUNTDOWN:

- Prepare ingredients.
- Microwave rice.
- Make chicken.

TARRAGON HERBED CHICKEN

3 tablespoons fresh tarragon OR 1 teaspoon dried tarragon
3/4 cup fresh parsley leaves
3/4 cup sliced baby bello mushrooms
Olive oil spray
3 pounds boneless, skinless chicken breast cutlets (about 1/2 inch thick)
1/2 teaspoon salt
1/4 teaspoon freshly ground black pepper
1 tablespoon olive oil
1 clove garlic, crushed

1. Coarsely chop tarragon, parsley, and mushrooms together in a food processor or by hand. Set aside.

2. Heat 2 large nonstick skillets over medium-high heat and spray each one with olive oil spray.

3. Divide the chicken between the two skillets and brown 2 minutes. Turn chicken and brown 2 more minutes. A meat thermometer inserted into chicken should read 165°F. Remove from pan.

4. Divide half of the chicken among 4 dinner plates. Sprinkle with salt and pepper. Place second half of the chicken on a plate, cover, and store in the refrigerator for Thursday night's dinner.

5. Add the olive oil to one skillet along with the chopped herbs and mushrooms and the garlic. Toss to warm through, about 1 minute. Spoon over the plated chicken.

BROWN RICE

Microwaveable brown rice (to make 3 cups cooked rice)
4 cups diced green bell pepper
4 teaspoons olive oil
1/2 teaspoon salt
1/4 teaspoon freshly ground black pepper

1. Microwave rice according to package instructions. Measure 3 cups rice. Store any leftover rice in the refrigerator for another meal.

2. Add diced green bell pepper, oil, and salt and pepper to the rice. Toss well and serve.

COST OF MEAL
PER PERSON
$4.65

PER SERVING

CHOICES/EXCHANGES
2 starch, 1/2 carbohydrate,
1 nonstarchy vegetable,
5 lean protein, 1 fat

Total Calories 510
Total Fat 16 g
Saturated Fat 2.7 g
Monounsaturated Fat 6.9 g
Trans Fat 0.0 g
Cholesterol 125 mg
Sodium 680 mg
Potassium 975 mg
Total Carbohydrate 45 g
Fiber 5 g
Sugars 3 g
Protein 44 g
Phosphorus 555 mg

WEDNESDAY NIGHT

TUNA SKILLET PIE

SERVES: 4

SERVING SIZE: 5 ounces tuna, 1 1/2 cups vegetables, 1 cup sauce, 6 tablespoons cheese, 3/4 cup linguine

PREP TIME: 10 minutes

COOKING TIME: 15 minutes

Skillet pie filled with tuna and pasta is a quick one-pot meal that's perfect for the midweek. Use the remaining tuna bought for Monday night's dinner in this recipe.

The smoky, sweet flavor of chipotle pepper, a dried and smoked jalapeño pepper, adds a special taste to this meal. Ground chipotle powder can be found in the spice section of the market.

The pasta in this recipe is cooked in the skillet with the other ingredients, so it's best to use fresh pasta.

HELPFUL HINTS:

- Any type of shredded, reduced-fat cheese you happen to have on hand can be used for the topping.
- Any type of mushrooms can be used.
- To save preparation time, use pre-chopped fresh onion and green bell pepper, which are often available in the produce section of the market.
- Use two skillets if you don't have a very large one.

COUNTDOWN:

- Prepare ingredients.
- Make recipe.

TUNA SKILLET PIE

4 teaspoons canola oil
1 1/2 cups diced onion
2 cups chopped red bell pepper
1/4 teaspoon chipotle powder
2 cups low-sodium tomato sauce*
2 cups water
1/2 pound fresh whole-wheat linguine
2 cups sliced baby bello mushrooms
1 1/2 pounds fresh tuna, cut into 1/2-inch pieces
1/4 teaspoon salt
1 1/2 cups shredded, reduced-fat sharp cheddar cheese

**Look for low-sodium, no-sugar added pasta sauce containing per 1 cup: 103 calories, 0.5 g fat, 21.3 g carbohydrate, 21 mg sodium.*

1. Heat oil in a large nonstick skillet over medium-high heat.

2. Add onion, green bell pepper, and chipotle powder, and sauté 3–4 minutes.

3. Add tomato sauce and water. Bring to simmer, add pasta, stir to mix it into the sauce, and cook gently 5 minutes.

4. Add mushrooms and tuna. Simmer 3 minutes. Add salt and sprinkle with cheese.

5. Remove from heat. Cover skillet with a lid and let sit 2–3 minutes to melt cheese. Bring skillet to the table and cut pie into wedges to serve.

COST OF MEAL
PER PERSON
$5.77

PER SERVING

CHOICES/EXCHANGES
2 1/2 starch, 4 nonstarchy vegetable, 6 lean protein

Total Calories 580
Total Fat 11 g
Saturated Fat 2.9 g
Monounsaturated Fat 4.3 g
Trans Fat 0.0 g
Cholesterol 85 mg
Sodium 600 mg
Potassium 965 mg
Total Carbohydrate 60 g
Fiber 9 g
Sugars 11 g
Protein 62 g
Phosphorus 490 mg

THURSDAY NIGHT

CHICKEN PANINI WITH ITALIAN SALAD

SERVES: 4

SERVING SIZE: 5 ounces chicken, 1 tablespoon mayonnaise, 1 1/2 tablespoons cheese, 2 tablespoons tarragon, 2 slices bread, 2 1/2 cups salad, 1 tablespoon dressing

PREP TIME: 5 minutes

COOKING TIME: 5 minutes

A panini with crisp bread, warm tasty filling, and melted cheese makes a perfect simple supper. If you don't have a panini press, simply place the sandwich in a sauté pan and press it down with a lid or another pan that fits inside.

Whole-wheat crusty bread is used for this panini. You can use a large baguette, Italian sub roll, or focaccia instead.

HELPFUL HINTS:

- Sauté the paninis over low heat so the insides will warm and the crust will be crisp and golden brown, not black.
- If you don't have a large nonstick skillet, use 2 skillets or make the paninis in batches.

COUNTDOWN:

- Assemble salad and set aside.
- Make paninis.

CHICKEN PANINI

8 slices crusty whole-wheat bread (about 1 ounce each)
4 tablespoons reduced-fat mayonnaise
1 1/2 pounds cooked chicken (saved from Tuesday night)
1/4 teaspoon salt
1/4 teaspoon freshly ground black pepper
6 ounces sliced, reduced fat Swiss cheese
1/2 cup fresh tarragon leaves
Olive oil spray

1. Place bread slices on a countertop and spread mayonnaise on 4 of the slices. Divide the chicken among the 4 remaining slices. Sprinkle with salt and pepper. Place Swiss cheese over the chicken. Place tarragon leaves over the cheese. Close the sandwiches with the 4 slices, mayonnaise side inside the sandwich.

2. Heat a large nonstick skillet (large enough to hold the paninis) over low heat and spray with olive oil spray. Add the paninis and press down with a lid or another clean pan. Cook for 2 minutes, turn, and press with a lid. Cook another 2 minutes. OR place paninis in a panini press and cook until the cheese is melted and bread is golden.

3. Cut each panini in half and serve with salad.

ITALIAN SALAD

8 cups washed, ready-to-eat Italian-style salad greens
2 cups fresh arugula
4 tablespoons reduce-fat oil and vinegar dressing*

1. Place Italian-style salad greens in a bowl.

2. Tear arugula into small pieces and add to bowl. Toss with dressing and serve.

**Look for reduced-fat oil and vinegar dressing containing per tablespoon: 11 calories, 1.0 g fat, 4 mg sodium.*

COST OF MEAL PER PERSON

$4.69

PER SERVING

CHOICES/EXCHANGES
2 starch, 1 nonstarchy vegetable, 7 lean protein, 1/2 fat

Total Calories 520
Total Fat 16 g
Saturated Fat 3.8 g
Monounsaturated Fat 5.0 g
Trans Fat 0.0 g
Cholesterol 140 mg
Sodium 560 mg
Potassium 1080 mg
Total Carbohydrate 32 g
Fiber 6 g
Sugars 6 g
Protein 56 g
Phosphorus 785 mg

FRIDAY NIGHT

ONION, PEPPER, AND MUSHROOM PIZZA

SERVES: 4

SERVING SIZE: 2 slices pizza topped with 2 3/4 cups vegetables and 1 1/2 tablespoons cheese

PREP TIME: 5 minutes

COOKING TIME: 30 minutes

Here's a quick pizza dinner that takes less time to cook than sending out for one. Swiss cheese, mushrooms, peppers, tomatoes, and onions top a crisp thin-crust base. You can also use any leftover vegetables you may have on hand. When shopping, look for a whole-wheat, thin-crust pizza base.

The order in which you layer the toppings makes a difference in how fast the pizza cooks. I place the peppers and onions on top so that they are exposed to the heat and will cook through in 25 minutes.

HELPFUL HINTS:

- Red onion can be used instead of Vidalia onions.
- Whole-grain French bread or whole-wheat pita bread can be used as a pizza base if you can't find one.

COUNTDOWN:

- Preheat oven to 400°F.
- Prepare pizza.
- Bake pizza.

ONION, PEPPER, AND MUSHROOM PIZZA

1 (12-inch) whole-wheat, thin-crust pizza base (such as Boboli brand)
Olive oil spray
3 ripe tomatoes, sliced (about 3 cups)
2 teaspoons dried oregano
6 ounces sliced, reduced-fat Swiss cheese
4 cups sliced baby bello mushrooms
2 cups thinly sliced bell peppers (red, yellow, or green)
2 cups thinly sliced Vidalia onion or other sweet onion

1. Preheat oven to 400°F.

2. Line a baking sheet with foil. Place pizza base on the foil and spray with olive oil spray. Place sliced tomatoes on top. Sprinkle oregano over tomatoes. Place Swiss cheese slices over tomatoes. Spread mushrooms over the cheese and bell peppers and onions on top of the mushrooms.

3. Place on the middle shelf of the oven for 25 minutes.

4. Remove from oven. Cut into 8 slices and serve.

COST OF MEAL
PER PERSON
$3.45

PER SERVING

CHOICES/EXCHANGES
2 1/2 starch, 3 nonstarchy vegetable, 1 lean protein, 1 fat

Total Calories 350
Total Fat 9 g
Saturated Fat 3.1 g
Monounsaturated Fat 3.5 g
Trans Fat 0.0 g
Cholesterol 15 mg
Sodium 440 mg
Potassium 825 mg
Total Carbohydrate 51 g
Fiber 11 g
Sugars 13 g
Protein 24 g
Phosphorus 375 mg

SATURDAY NIGHT

SPICED LAMB STEAK WITH FLORENTINE RICE

SERVES: 4
SERVING SIZE: 5 ounces lamb, 1 teaspoon spice mixture, 3/4 cup rice, 2 1/2 cups spinach, 1 teaspoon oil
PREP TIME: 5 minutes
COOKING TIME: 15 minutes

A steak cut from the leg of the lamb is tender and juicy and cooks in just minutes. The spiced coating in this recipe makes the dish special with little effort. If you don't see lamb steaks in the meat case, ask the butcher for 4 steaks about 1/2–3/4 inch thick cut from the leg of lamb. The steak is cut straight through the leg making a round steak with a small bone in the center.

HELPFUL HINTS:

- Dried spices keep for about 6 months. Buy new spices if yours are older.
- The lamb steaks should be in one layer in the skillet. If your skillet is not large enough, use 2 skillets.

COUNTDOWN:

- Make lamb.
- While lamb cooks, make rice.

SPICED LAMB STEAK

4 (6-ounce) lamb steaks center cut from leg
2 teaspoons ground allspice
2 teaspoons ground cinnamon
1/4 teaspoon cayenne pepper
Olive oil spray

1. Remove visible fat from lamb.

2. Mix allspice, cinnamon, and cayenne pepper together in a small bowl. Spread mixture on both sides of lamb steaks.

3. Heat a large nonstick skillet over medium-high heat and spray with olive oil spray. Add the lamb and brown 2 minutes. Turn and brown 2 more minutes. Lower heat to medium, cover with a lid, and cook 5 minutes. A meat thermometer inserted into lamb should read 125°F for rare, 145°F for medium.

FLORENTINE RICE

10 cups washed, ready-to-eat spinach
Microwaveable brown rice (to make 3 cups cooked rice)
4 teaspoons olive oil
1/2 teaspoon salt
1/4 teaspoon freshly ground black pepper

1. Place spinach in a large, microwave-safe bowl and microwave on high 1 minute.

2. Remove spinach from microwave and cook rice in the microwave according to package instructions. Measure 3 cups of rice and reserve any remaining rice for another dinner.

3. Add rice to the spinach and toss with olive oil, and salt and pepper.

COST OF MEAL PER PERSON

$4.21

PER SERVING

CHOICES/EXCHANGES
2 starch, 2 nonstarchy vegetable, 4 lean protein, 2 fat

Total Calories 500
Total Fat 18 g
Saturated Fat 4.5 g
Monounsaturated Fat 7.7 g
Trans Fat 0.0 g
Cholesterol 110 mg
Sodium 470 mg
Potassium 1055 mg
Total Carbohydrate 44 g
Fiber 5 g
Sugars 1 g
Protein 41 g
Phosphorus 520 mg

WEEK **NINE**

WEEKLY BUDGET
Average cost of a meal per person for the week is
$5.47

SUNDAY NIGHT

BALSAMIC PORK SCALOPPINI WITH GARLIC SWEET POTATOES AND SUGAR SNAP PEAS

Pork tenderloin cut into thin scaloppini is served with a sauce of sweet and tart balsamic vinegar and topped with pine nuts. Garlic flavors the sweet potatoes and sugar snap peas. They take only minutes to prepare in a microwave oven.

MONDAY NIGHT

CHICKEN PICADILLO WITH BROWN RICE

Capers and raisins lend a sweet and savory flavor to this popular Latin dish. Ground chicken, onion, green bell pepper, and tomato sauce are sautéed and served over rice.

TUESDAY NIGHT

MU SHU PORK WRAP WITH STIR-FRIED BOK CHOY

This is a classic Mandarin Chinese dish. For this dinner, pork is stir-fried with a ginger, garlic, soy sauce, and sherry mixture and shredded cabbage and then rolled in a wrap. Crunchy bok choy is stir-fried with peanuts to go with the wrap.

WEDNESDAY NIGHT

BASIL SHRIMP PASTA AND ITALIAN SALAD WITH PINE NUTS

Fresh basil and Parmesan cheese top shrimp cooked in pasta sauce in this midweek dinner. A surprise of grated orange rind adds sweetness and intrigue to the sauce. An Italian salad completes the meal.

THURSDAY NIGHT

CHICKEN TACOS WITH PINTO BEAN SALAD

These tacos are made with ground chicken marinated in a sauce of cumin and orange juice. Pinto beans are tossed with celery and cilantro for a tasty side salad.

FRIDAY NIGHT

VEGETABLE CASSEROLE SOUP

This is a hearty soup that uses leftover vegetables and herbs from this week's shopping. A mixture of horseradish and vinegar brightens the soup, and it's topped with cheddar cheese.

SATURDAY NIGHT

PERNOD SHRIMP WITH TOMATO RICE

Pernod, an anise-flavored liqueur, is the base for the cream sauce that coats the shrimp in this dish. The shrimp are served over a bed of brown rice and cubed tomatoes.

SHOPPING LIST

Here is the Shopping List for this week's dinners.

This shopping list will help you get in and out of the market quickly. The ingredients are listed by supermarket department to make shopping easier; you won't forget something in one department and have to go back and forth across the store.

The amount needed of each ingredient is listed so you will know what size package or can to buy. If it helps you to better visualize the amount you need, please note that 4 tablespoons equal 1/4 cup and 8 tablespoons equal 1/2 cup.

Make sure to check your refrigerator and pantry to see if you have any of these ingredients on hand before making your trip to the market.

MEAT AND SEAFOOD

3 pounds frozen, shelled large shrimp (wild caught or local)
2 1/2 pounds ground white meat chicken (no skin included)
3 pounds pork tenderloin

DAIRY

1 small carton light cream (4 tablespoons needed)
1 small package shredded, reduced-fat cheddar cheese (1 cup needed)
1 package shredded, reduced-fat Monterey Jack cheese (1/4 cup needed)
1 carton reduced-fat sour cream (1/4 cup needed)
1 small piece Parmesan cheese (4 tablespoons needed)

BAKERY

1 package 8-inch whole-wheat tortillas (8 needed)

SHOP SMART

- Look for canned low-sodium tomato sauce, containing per cup: 103 calories, 0.5 g fat, 21.3 g carbohydrate, 27 mg sodium.
- Look for canned low-sodium diced tomatoes, containing per cup: 41 calories, 0.3 g fat, 9.6 g carbohydrate, 24 mg sodium.
- Low-sodium, no-sugar added pasta sauce containing per cup (8 ounces): 131 calories, 3.8 g fat, 20.7 g carbohydrate, 77 mg sodium.
- Look for reduced-fat oil and vinegar dressing containing per tablespoon: 11 calories, 1.0 g fat, 4 mg sodium.

CONDIMENTS

1 small bottle prepared horseradish (2 tablespoons needed)
1 small bottle hot pepper sauce (several drops needed)
1 small bottle reduced-sodium soy sauce (2 tablespoons needed)
1 small bottle hoisin sauce (2 tablespoons needed)
1 bottle low-sodium tomato sauce (2 cups needed) (see *Shop Smart*, opposite)
1 small bottle Worcestershire sauce (4 tablespoons needed)
1 bottle distilled white vinegar (4 tablespoons needed)
1 bottle balsamic vinegar (1 cup plus 2 tablespoons needed)
1 bottle sesame oil (8 teaspoons needed)

SPICES

1 small bottle cayenne pepper (1/8 teaspoon needed)
1 small bottle ground cumin (2 teaspoons needed)

CANNED FOODS

1 large can low-sodium diced tomatoes (4 cups needed) (see *Shop Smart*, opposite)
1 can low-sodium pinto beans (4 3/4 cups rinsed and drained needed)
1 bottle low-sodium pasta sauce (2 cups needed (see *Shop Smart*, opposite)
1 small bottle orange juice (1/2 cup needed)
1 small bottle capers (4 tablespoons needed)
1 container fat-free, no-salt-added chicken broth (2 cups needed)

WINE AND SPIRITS

1 small bottle Pernod (1/2 cup needed)
1 small bottle dry sherry (2 tablespoons needed)

RICE AND PASTA

Microwaveable brown rice (to make 5 1/2 cups cooked rice)
1 small package whole-wheat rotelli (corkscrew) pasta (2 1/2 cups needed)

NUTS AND DRIED FRUIT

1 small package pine nuts (1/2 cup needed)
1 container dry-roasted, unsalted peanuts (4 tablespoons needed)
1 small package raisins (5 tablespoons needed)

PRODUCE

1 bunch celery (4 cups sliced needed)
1 large bok choy (8 cups sliced needed)
1 fennel bulb (4 cups sliced needed)
1 package ready-to-eat shredded cabbage (4 cups needed)
1 small piece fresh ginger (2 tablespoons grated needed)
1 green bell pepper (1 cup needed)
1 package green beans (1 cup needed)
1 bag washed, ready-to-eat Italian-style salad greens (4 cups needed)
1 container sliced mushrooms (2 cups needed)
7 medium onions (6 3/4 cups needed)
1 orange
1 package shredded romaine or iceberg lettuce (1 cup needed)
1/2 pound sugar snap peas
1 package washed, ready-to-eat spinach (4 cups needed)
1 bunch scallions (1 cup sliced needed)
1 bunch fresh cilantro (1/2 cup needed)
1 bunch fresh basil (2 cups needed)
1 bunch fresh tarragon (2 tablespoons needed; or dried tarragon can be used)
1 1/2 pounds sweet potatoes
3 tomatoes (3 cups needed)

STAPLES

Canola oil
Olive oil
Olive oil spray
1 head garlic (14 cloves needed)
Reduced-fat oil and vinegar dressing (see *Shop Smart*, opposite)
Salt
Black peppercorns

SUNDAY NIGHT

BALSAMIC PORK SCALOPPINI WITH GARLIC SWEET POTATOES AND SUGAR SNAP PEAS

SERVES: 4

SERVING SIZE: 5 ounces pork, 1/2 cup onion, 1/4 cup sauce, 1 tablespoon pine nuts, 3/4 cup sugar snap peas, 3/4 cup potatoes, 1 teaspoon olive oil

PREP TIME: 15 minutes

COOKING TIME: 20 minutes

Sweet and tart balsamic vinegar dresses up pork scaloppini. Sweet potato sticks and sugar snap peas add a colorful side dish to this meal.

There are many different qualities of balsamic vinegar. The best ones are made only from grapes; lesser ones add brown sugar or caramel. Read the label. It should say balsamic vinegar and not have any other added ingredients such as sugar.

Using the microwave helps speed the cooking of the potatoes and snap peas. Another time-saving tip is to use the dish they're microwaved in as a serving dish, which can be washed in the dishwasher; that's one less dish to clean! I have also given instructions for a stove-top method of cooking the vegetables.

HELPFUL HINTS:

- Thin-cut boneless pork chops can be used instead of pork tenderloin.
- Green beans or snow peas can be substituted for sugar snap peas. The cooking time and method are the same.
- Use 2 skillets if you don't have one large enough to fit all of the pork.

COUNTDOWN:

- Microwave potatoes and sugar snap peas and set aside.
- Make pork.
- Remove pork from skillet and sauté potatoes and sugar snap peas in the same skillet.

BALSAMIC PORK SCALOPPINI

1 1/2 pounds pork tenderloin
Olive oil spray
2 cups diced onion
1/4 teaspoon salt
1/4 teaspoon freshly ground black pepper
1 cup balsamic vinegar
1/4 cup pine nuts
1/4 cup chopped cilantro

1. Remove fat from pork tenderloin and cut into 2-inch slices. Flatten the slices with a meat bat or the bottom of a clean, heavy skillet to about 1/2-inch thickness.

2. Heat a nonstick skillet over medium-high heat. Spray with olive oil spray. Add onion and sauté 3 minutes. Move onion to the sides of the skillet.

3. Add pork to the skillet and sauté 2 minutes per side. Remove to a plate; sprinkle with salt and pepper.

4. Raise heat under the skillet to high and add vinegar. Reduce liquid by half, about 1 minute. Add pine nuts and warm through, about 30 seconds.

5. Divide pork among 4 dinner plates and spoon sauce and pine nuts on top. Sprinkle cilantro on top.

GARLIC SWEET POTATOES AND SUGAR SNAP PEAS

1 pound sweet potatoes (about 3 1/2 cups strips)
1/2 pound sugar snap peas, trimmed (about 3 1/2 cups)
4 teaspoons olive oil
4 medium cloves garlic, crushed
1/2 teaspoon salt
1/4 teaspoon freshly ground black pepper

1. Wash potatoes. Peel and cut them into strips about the same size as the sugar snap peas (about 2 inches × 1/2 inch).

2. ***Microwave method:*** Place potatoes and sugar snap peas in a bowl and cook in a microwave oven on high for 5 minutes. ***Stove-top method:*** Bring a saucepan of water to a boil and add the potatoes. Boil 3 minutes, add sugar snap peas, and boil 2 more minutes. Drain.

3. When the pork is cooked and removed from skillet, add the oil and garlic to the same skillet used for the pork. Add the potatoes and snow peas. Toss for 2–3 minutes or until potatoes are crisp and cooked through. Sprinkle with salt and pepper and serve.

COST OF MEAL PER PERSON
$4.63

PER SERVING

CHOICES/EXCHANGES
1 1/2 starch, 1 carbohydrate, 2 nonstarchy vegetable, 5 lean protein, 1 fat

Total Calories 500
Total Fat 14 g
Saturated Fat 2.6 g
Monounsaturated Fat 6.2 g
Trans Fat 0.0 g
Cholesterol 110 mg
Sodium 620 mg
Potassium 1420 mg
Total Carbohydrate 48 g
Fiber 7 g
Sugars 20 g
Protein 41 g
Phosphorus 545 mg

MONDAY NIGHT

CHICKEN PICADILLO WITH BROWN RICE

SERVES: 4
SERVING SIZE: 5 ounces ground chicken, 1/2 cup vegetables, 1/2 cup sauce, 1/2 cup plus 2 tablespoons rice
PREP TIME: 15 minutes
COOKING TIME: 15 minutes

Picadillo is a popular Latin dish using ground meat, onions, green bell pepper, tomato sauce, capers, and raisins. The success of this dish is in the blending of sweet and savory flavors. Rice is the traditional side dish with picadillo.

HELPFUL HINTS:

- Frozen chopped onion and green bell pepper can be used instead of fresh to cut down on preparation time.

COUNTDOWN:

- Start picadillo.
- Make rice.
- Finish picadillo.

CHICKEN PICADILLO

2 teaspoons canola oil
1 cup diced onion
1 cup diced green bell pepper
3 medium cloves garlic, crushed
1 1/2 pounds ground white meat chicken (no skin included)
2 cups low-sodium tomato sauce*
4 tablespoons Worcestershire sauce
4 tablespoons capers
5 tablespoons raisins
4 tablespoons distilled white vinegar
1/4 teaspoon salt
1/4 teaspoon freshly ground black pepper

1. Heat oil in a large nonstick skillet over medium-high heat. Add the onions, green pepper, garlic, and ground chicken. Sauté 3–4 minutes, breaking up the chicken into small pieces as it cooks.

2. Add the tomato sauce and sauté until the sauce starts to bubble, about 2–3 minutes. Add the Worcestershire, capers, raisins, and vinegar.

3. Reduce heat to medium and cook gently about 3–4 minutes. Add salt and pepper and serve with rice.

**Look for low-sodium tomato sauce, containing per cup (8 ounces): 103 calories, 0.5 g fat, 21.3 g carbohydrate, 21 mg sodium.*

BROWN RICE

Microwaveable brown rice (to make 2 1/2 cups cooked rice)
2 teaspoons canola oil

1. Microwave rice according to package instructions. Measure 2 1/2 cups rice and reserve any remaining rice for another dinner.

2. Add oil to rice and toss.

COST OF MEAL PER PERSON

$ 4.88

PER SERVING

CHOICES/EXCHANGES
2 starch, 1/2 fruit,
1/2 carbohydrate,
3 nonstarchy vegetable,
5 lean protein

Total Calories 510
Total Fat 11 g
Saturated Fat 1.7 g
Monounsaturated Fat 4.5 g
Trans Fat 0.0 g
Cholesterol 125 mg
Sodium 580 mg
Potassium 1370 mg
Total Carbohydrate 59 g
Fiber 6 g
Sugars 18 g
Protein 45 g
Phosphorus 565 mg

TUESDAY NIGHT

MU SHU PORK WRAP WITH STIR-FRIED BOK CHOY

SERVES: 4
SERVING SIZE: 5 ounces pork, 1 tablespoon sauce, 1 1/4 cups vegetables, 1/2 tablespoon hoisin sauce, 1 whole-wheat tortilla, 2 cups bok choy, 1 tablespoon peanuts, 2 teaspoons sesame oil
PREP TIME: 15 minutes
COOKING TIME: 15 minutes

This is a quick take on a popular Chinese classic. This dish is made with sautéed pork tenderloin and shredded cabbage, which cook in just a few minutes in a hot wok. I have used whole-wheat tortillas as the wrap. Fresh bok choy is stir-fried for a few minutes as a side dish to complete the meal. I use the same wok to prepare both the pork and the side dish.

HELPFUL HINTS:

- Ready-to-eat shredded cabbage for coleslaw can be found in the produce section.
- Chinese cabbage (also called napa cabbage) can be used instead of bok choy.

COUNTDOWN:

- Prepare all ingredients.
- Marinate pork.
- Stir-fry bok choy.
- Complete pork dish using the same wok.

MU SHU PORK WRAP

1 1/2 pounds pork tenderloin
3 cloves garlic, crushed
2 tablespoons grated or chopped fresh ginger
2 tablespoons reduced-sodium soy sauce
2 tablespoons dry sherry
4 teaspoons sesame oil
4 cups ready-to-eat shredded cabbage
1 cup sliced scallions
1/4 teaspoon freshly ground black pepper
2 tablespoons hoisin sauce
4 (8-inch) whole-wheat tortillas

1. Remove visible fat from pork and cut into strips about 1/4 inch thick. Mix garlic, ginger, soy sauce, and sherry together in a bowl, add the pork strips and set aside to marinate.

2. In the same wok or skillet used for the bok choy heat oil until smoking, and add the cabbage and scallions. Stir-fry 1 minute.

3. Push cabbage to the sides of the pan and add the pork and sauce. Stir-fry 3 minutes in the center of the pan. Draw in the cabbage and continue to cook 1 minute. Add pepper and stir.

4. Spread hoisin sauce on tortillas. Add pork and vegetables. Roll up and place seam side down on 4 plates. Cut in half and serve with bok choy.

STIR-FRIED BOK CHOY

4 teaspoons sesame oil
8 cups sliced bok choy
4 tablespoons dry-roasted, unsalted peanuts

1. Heat oil in a wok or large skillet until smoking. Add the bok choy. Stir-fry 3–4 minutes. Add the peanuts and stir.

2. Remove to 4 dinner plates and use the same wok to cook the pork.

COST OF MEAL
PER PERSON
$4.68

PER SERVING

CHOICES/EXCHANGES
1 1/2 starch, 1 nonstarchy vegetable, 6 lean protein, 1 1/2 fat

Total Calories 480
Total Fat 20 g
Saturated Fat 3.9 g
Monounsaturated Fat 7.4 g
Trans Fat 0.0 g
Cholesterol 110 mg
Sodium 690 mg
Potassium 1395 mg
Total Carbohydrate 31 g
Fiber 7 g
Sugars 8 g
Protein 45 g
Phosphorus 630 mg

WEDNESDAY NIGHT

BASIL SHRIMP PASTA AND ITALIAN SALAD WITH PINE NUTS

SERVES: 4

SERVING SIZE: 5 ounces shrimp, 3/4 cup sauce, 1/2 cup basil, 5 tablespoons onion, 1/2 cup pasta, 1 teaspoon oil, 1 tablespoon Parmesan cheese, 1 cup salad, 1 tablespoon pine nuts, 1 tablespoon dressing

PREP TIME: 15 minutes

COOKING TIME: 20 minutes

Orange peel adds intriguing flavor to this shrimp and tomato pasta dish. The shrimp cook quickly in the tomato and orange sauce, and are served over a bed of rotelli (corkscrew) pasta. Fresh basil and Parmesan cheese finish the dish. An Italian salad completes this colorful meal.

HELPFUL HINTS:

- Use a potato peeler to peel orange strips. Try not to take any white pith with the peel.
- Any short cut pasta such as penne or bowtie can be used.
- Any type of pasta sauce can be used for this dish.
- A quick way to chop fresh basil is to snip the leaves with a scissors.

COUNTDOWN:

- Place a large pot of water for the pasta on to boil.
- Make salad and set aside.
- Make the shrimp dish.

BASIL SHRIMP PASTA

4 teaspoons olive oil
1 1/4 cups sliced onion
4 cloves garlic, crushed
2 cups low-sodium pasta sauce*
1 cup water
6 strips orange peel, about 2 inches × 1/2 inch
1 1/2 pounds frozen, shelled large shrimp, defrosted
1/8 teaspoon cayenne pepper
1/2 teaspoon salt
1/4 teaspoon freshly ground black pepper
2 cups chopped fresh basil
2 1/2 cups whole-wheat rotelli (corkscrew) pasta
4 tablespoons freshly grated Parmesan cheese

**Look for low-sodium pasta sauce containing per 1/2 cup: 112 calories, 3.5 g fat, 17.7 g carbohydrate, 39 mg sodium.*

1. Fill a large saucepan with water and bring to a boil for the pasta.

2. Heat oil in a large nonstick skillet over medium-high heat. Add onion and sauté 3 minutes without browning. Add garlic and sauté another 1 minute. Add pasta sauce, water, and orange peel and cook 7–8 minutes.

3. Lower heat to medium and add shrimp and cayenne pepper. Cook gently 2–3 minutes, turning shrimp over until shrimp are pink. Add salt and pepper. Remove orange peel and stir in basil.

4. While sauce cooks, add pasta to the boiling water and cook for 8 minutes or according to package instructions; drain and divide among 4 dinner plates.

5. Spoon shrimp and sauce over the cooked pasta, sprinkle with Parmesan cheese, and serve.

ITALIAN SALAD WITH PINE NUTS

4 cups washed, ready-to-eat Italian-style salad greens
1/4 cup pine nuts
4 tablespoons reduced-fat oil and vinegar dressing**

1. Place salad greens in a bowl. Add the pine nuts and toss with the dressing.

***Look for reduced-fat oil and vinegar dressing containing per tablespoon: 11 calories, 1.0 g fat, 4 mg sodium.*

COST OF MEAL PER PERSON

$7.85

PER SERVING

CHOICES/EXCHANGES
3 starch, 2 nonstarchy vegetable, 5 lean protein, 1/2 fat

Total Calories 520
Total Fat 14 g
Saturated Fat 2.7 g
Monounsaturated Fat 5.0 g
Trans Fat 0.0 g
Cholesterol 285 mg
Sodium 640 mg
Potassium 1355 mg
Total Carbohydrate 56 g
Fiber 10 g
Sugars 11 g
Protein 47 g
Phosphorus 650 mg

THURSDAY NIGHT

CHICKEN TACOS WITH PINTO BEAN SALAD

SERVES: 4
SERVING SIZE: 3 1/2 ounces ground chicken, 1 ounce orange juice, 1 whole-wheat tortilla, 1 tablespoon cheese, 1/2 cup vegetables, 1 tablespoon sour cream, 1 cup salad, 1 tablespoon dressing
PREP TIME: 15 minutes
COOKING TIME: 20 minutes

Tacos are becoming one of America's favorite foods. Tacos—tortillas folded in half and filled with meat and vegetables—are made with either corn or flour tortillas. For this quick dinner, I use whole-wheat flour tortillas. To save preparation time, use fresh diced tomatoes and celery already prepared from the produce department in the supermarket. Packaged shredded cheese and lettuce also save preparation time.

HELPFUL HINTS:

- Look for ground white-meat-only chicken without added skin.
- Any type of shredded, reduced-fat cheese can be used.
- Any rinsed and drained canned beans can be used, such as black beans or red kidney beans, for the salad.

COUNTDOWN:

- Marinate chicken.
- Make Pinto Bean Salad.
- Finish tacos.

CHICKEN TACOS

2 teaspoons ground cumin
1/2 cup orange juice
Several drops hot pepper sauce
1 pound ground white meat chicken (no skin included)
4 (8-inch) whole-wheat flour tortillas
1/4 cup shredded, reduced-fat Monterey Jack cheese
1 cup shredded romaine or iceberg lettuce
1 cup diced tomatoes
1/4 cup reduced-fat sour cream

1. Mix cumin, orange juice, and hot pepper sauce together in a bowl. Add the chicken and stir to make sure all the chicken is covered by the marinade. Leave in the marinade while preparing the remaining taco ingredients.

2. Heat a nonstick skillet over medium-high heat and add the chicken and marinade. Sauté 3–4 minutes, breaking up the chicken into small pieces as it cooks.

3. Wrap tortillas in a paper towel. Microwave on high 30 seconds. Remove and place the tortillas on a counter.

4. Divide the cheese among the 4 tortillas. Add the chicken over the cheese and then add the lettuce and tomatoes. Top each taco with a spoonful of sour cream. Fold the tortillas in half. Serve extra hot pepper sauce on the side, if desired.

PINTO BEAN SALAD

4 tablespoons reduced-fat oil and vinegar dressing*
2 cups rinsed and drained canned pinto beans
2 cups sliced celery
4 tablespoons chopped cilantro
1/2 teaspoon salt
1/4 teaspoon freshly ground black pepper

1. Add the dressing and beans to a bowl. Add celery, cilantro, salt, and pepper. Toss well and serve.

**Look for reduced-fat oil and vinegar dressing containing per tablespoon: 11 calories, 1.0 g fat, 4 mg sodium.*

COST OF MEAL PER PERSON

$3.57

PER SERVING

CHOICES/EXCHANGES
2 1/2 starch,
1 nonstarchy vegetable,
4 lean protein

Total Calories 400
Total Fat 9 g
Saturated Fat 3.5 g
Monounsaturated Fat 2.3 g
Trans Fat 0.0 g
Cholesterol 95 mg
Sodium 670 mg
Potassium 1155 mg
Total Carbohydrate 41 g
Fiber 9 g
Sugars 8 g
Protein 37 g
Phosphorus 520 mg

FRIDAY NIGHT

VEGETABLE CASSEROLE SOUP

SERVES: 4
SERVING SIZE: 2 1/2 cups vegetables, 3/4 cup beans, 1/2 cup potatoes, 1/4 cup cheese, 1 cup liquid
PREP TIME: 15 minutes
COOKING TIME: 20 minutes

Use the remaining vegetables and herbs from this week's shopping trip to make this hearty soup. It's a whole meal in one bowl! The horseradish and vinegar add a little kick and help the flavors of the vegetables blend. The cheddar cheese adds flavor and texture. You can make this a vegetarian meal by using vegetable broth instead of chicken broth.

HELPFUL HINTS:

- Any type of low-fat cheese can be substituted for the cheddar cheese.
- To save time, slice all of the vegetables in a food processor fitted with a thick slicing blade.
- A few drops of hot pepper sauce can be used instead of horseradish.

COUNTDOWN:

- Make soup.

VEGETABLE CASSEROLE SOUP

2 tablespoons canola oil
1 1/2 cups sliced onion
2 cups sliced celery
2 cups sliced mushrooms
2 cups fat-free, no-salt-added chicken broth
4 cups canned low-sodium diced tomatoes (including juice)*
1 cup green beans, cut into 2-inch pieces
2 cups chopped peeled sweet potatoes (1-inch pieces)
2 tablespoons horseradish
2 tablespoons balsamic vinegar
4 cups washed, ready-to-eat spinach
2 3/4 cups rinsed and drained canned pinto beans
1/4 teaspoon freshly ground black pepper
1 cup shredded, reduced-fat cheddar cheese

1. Heat oil in a large casserole or saucepan over medium-high heat. Add the onion, celery, and mushrooms. Sauté 3–4 minutes without browning the onion. Add the chicken broth and canned tomatoes and bring to a simmer.

2. Add the green beans and sweet potatoes. Cover with a lid, lower heat to medium, and cook on a slow boil 10 minutes.

3. Mix horseradish and vinegar together in a small bowl. Add to soup with the spinach and pinto beans. Cover and boil 2 minutes. Spinach will be just wilted. Add pepper and stir.

4. Divide the soup among 4 large soup bowls. Sprinkle cheese on top and serve.

**Look for canned low-sodium diced tomatoes, containing per cup: 41 calories, 0.3 g fat, 9.6 g carbohydrate, 24 mg sodium.*

COST OF MEAL
PER PERSON

$3.32

PER SERVING

CHOICES/EXCHANGES
2 1/2 starch,
4 nonstarchy vegetable,
1 lean protein, 1 1/2 fat

Total Calories 410
Total Fat 11 g
Saturated Fat 2.1 g
Monounsaturated Fat 5.2 g
Trans Fat 0.0 g
Cholesterol 5 mg
Sodium 630 mg
Potassium 1860 mg
Total Carbohydrate 60 g
Fiber 18 g
Sugars 17 g
Protein 23 g
Phosphorus 510 mg

SATURDAY NIGHT

PERNOD SHRIMP WITH TOMATO RICE

SERVES: 4
SERVING SIZE: 5 ounces shrimp,
1 1/4 cups vegetables, 1/4 cup sauce,
1 1/2 teaspoons tarragon, 3/4 cup rice,
1/2 cup tomatoes, 2 teaspoons oil
PREP TIME: 15 minutes
COOKING TIME: 15 minutes

The shrimp in this dish is cooked in Pernod, an anise-flavored liqueur. Pernod is also excellent for flavoring other shellfish. No need to buy a large bottle; small bottles (airline size or splits) are available in most liquor stores. Tarragon, which is also used in this recipe, has an anise flavor as well.

HELPFUL HINTS:

- Ouzo and Ricard are anise-flavored liqueurs and can be used instead of Pernod.
- Dry vermouth can be used instead of Pernod. The flavor of the dish will be different, but still very good.
- If fennel isn't available, use sliced celery instead.

COUNTDOWN:

- Make rice and set aside.
- Make shrimp.

PERNOD SHRIMP

4 teaspoons canola oil
1 cup coarsely chopped onion
4 cups sliced fennel bulb
1 1/2 pounds frozen, shelled large shrimp, defrosted
1/2 cup Pernod
4 tablespoons water
4 tablespoons light cream
1/4 teaspoon salt
1/4 teaspoon freshly ground black pepper
2 tablespoons chopped fresh tarragon OR 1 teaspoon dried

1. Heat oil in a nonstick skillet over medium-high heat. Add the onion and fennel and sauté 5 minutes, stirring once or twice. Add shrimp and sauté another minute, tossing them in the pan.

2. Pour in the Pernod and cook to reduce, about 1 minute. Add water and let shrimp simmer 2–3 minutes or until they turn pink. Remove shrimp with a slotted spoon.

3. Raise the heat under the skillet and reduce the juices in the pan by half. Add the cream and cook on low heat for 1 minute.

4. Return shrimp to the pan and turn over in the sauce just to warm them. Add salt and pepper. Divide among 4 dinner plates. Sprinkle tarragon on top and serve.

TOMATO RICE

Microwaveable brown rice (to make 3 cups cooked rice)
2 tomatoes, cut into cubes (about 2 cups)
4 teaspoons canola oil
1/4 teaspoon salt
1/4 teaspoon freshly ground black pepper

1. Cook rice according to package instructions. Measure 3 cups and reserve any remaining rice for another dinner.

2. Add the tomato cubes, olive oil, salt, and pepper. Toss and serve with the shrimp.

COST OF MEAL PER PERSON
$9.38

PER SERVING

CHOICES/EXCHANGES
2 starch, 1 carbohydrate,
2 nonstarchy vegetable,
5 lean protein, 1 fat

Total Calories 570
Total Fat 15 g
Saturated Fat 3.1 g
Monounsaturated Fat 7.3 g
Trans Fat 0.0 g
Cholesterol 285 mg
Sodium 560 mg
Potassium 880 mg
Total Carbohydrate 53 g
Fiber 7 g
Sugars 5 g
Protein 41 g
Phosphorus 570 mg

WEEK **TEN**

WEEKLY BUDGET
Average cost of a meal per person for the week is
$5.43

SUNDAY NIGHT
VEAL MEAT LOAF WITH ORANGE BARLEY
Onion, celery, carrots, and mushrooms added to ground veal make a light, delicious meat loaf. Orange juice flavors the 10-minute barley side dish for this meal.

MONDAY NIGHT
BUFFALO CHICKEN LEGS WITH BLUE CHEESE SALAD
Sweet and spicy chicken drumsticks are served with a cool salad topped with blue cheese dressing in this quick Monday night meal.

TUESDAY NIGHT
LEMON PEPPER SCALLOPS AND COUSCOUS WITH GREEN BEANS AND HERBED GOAT CHEESE
Sweet sea scallops are served with a hot and tangy sauce made from lemon juice and cracked black pepper in this dish. The couscous side dish is packed with herbs from the goat cheese and fresh basil.

WEDNESDAY NIGHT
PANZANELLA SALAD (TUSCAN TOMATO AND BREAD SALAD)
Use up 2-day-old bread in this traditional Tuscan salad. It's tossed with fresh ingredients like tomatoes, basil, cucumber, and black olives. Reserved cooked chicken from Monday night completes the salad.

THURSDAY NIGHT
QUICK-FRIED DICED VEAL WITH SIMPLE FRIED RICE
Stir-fry veal and snow peas for an unbelievably easy Chinese dinner. Microwaved brown rice is added to the wok after the veal is removed to pick up the wok flavor for the fried rice side dish.

FRIDAY NIGHT
MEXICAN FIESTA BOWL
Avocado, black beans, corn, tomato, and brown rice make a colorful vegetarian meal in a bowl. This refreshing one-bowl meal is topped with sliced almonds and cilantro.

SATURDAY NIGHT
PAN-SEARED SCALLOPS WITH VEGETABLE MEDLEY RICE
These scallops only need a little olive oil and chopped chives for flavor. They cook in just 3 minutes! Sour cream is mixed with horseradish to make a peppery dressing for the brown rice, red bell pepper, and mushroom side dish.

SHOPPING LIST

Here is the Shopping List for this week's dinners.

This shopping list will help you get in and out of the market quickly. The ingredients are listed by supermarket department to make shopping easier; you won't forget something in one department and have to go back and forth across the store.

The amount needed of each ingredient is listed so you will know what size package or can to buy. If it helps you to better visualize the amount you need, please note that 4 tablespoons equal 1/4 cup and 8 tablespoons equal 1/2 cup.

Make sure to check your refrigerator and pantry to see if you have any of these ingredients on hand before making your trip to the market.

MEAT AND SEAFOOD
1 pound ground veal (see *Shop Smart*, opposite)
6 pounds skinless chicken drumsticks with bone
3 pounds frozen sea scallops (wild caught)
1 1/2 pounds veal cutlet

DAIRY
1 small package herbed goat cheese (1 ounce needed)
1 small carton reduced-fat sour cream (1/2 cup needed)

BAKERY
1 container whole-wheat bread crumbs (1/2 cup needed)
1 small container whole-wheat croutons (4 ounces needed)
1 loaf whole-grain bread (6 slices needed)

SHOP SMART

- Look for lean ground veal containing per ounce: 43 calories, 2 g fat, 1 g saturated fat.
- Look for reduced-fat oil and vinegar dressing containing per tablespoon: 11 calories, 1.0 g fat, 4 mg sodium.

CONDIMENTS

1 small bottle honey (6 tablespoons needed)
1 bottle distilled vinegar (8 tablespoons needed)
1 bottle low-calorie blue cheese dressing (8 tablespoons needed)
1 container pitted black olives (10 olives needed)
1 small bottle reduced-sodium soy sauce (4 tablespoons needed)
1 bottle sesame oil (5 tablespoons needed)
1 small bottle prepared horseradish (2 tablespoons needed)

SPICES

1 small bottle nutmeg (1/2 teaspoon needed)
1 small bottle cayenne pepper (1 teaspoon needed)
1 small bottle cracked black pepper (1 teaspoon needed)

CANNED FOODS AND FROZEN FOODS

1 small can tomato paste (8 tablespoons needed)
1 package frozen corn kernels (1 cup needed)
1 can low-sodium black beans (2 cups needed)
1 container fat-free, no-salt-added chicken broth (2 cups needed)

WINE AND SPIRITS

1 small bottle dry sherry (1/2 cup needed)

JUICE

1 small bottle orange juice (or 1 orange; 2 tablespoons juice needed)

RICE, PASTA, BARLEY, COUSCOUS

1 package quick-cooking pearl barley (1 cup needed)
1 small package precooked whole-grain couscous (1 cup needed)
Microwaveable brown rice (to make 7 cups cooked rice)

NUTS

1 small package pine nuts (1/2 cup needed)
1 small package sliced almonds (2 tablespoons needed)

PRODUCE

2 onions (2 cups needed)
1 bunch celery (1/2 cup needed)
1 package carrots (1/2 cup needed)
1 container sliced button mushrooms (3 cups needed)
1 bunch parsley (1 cup needed)
1 bunch basil (2 1/2 cups needed)
1 bunch cilantro (1/2 cup needed)
1 bunch chives (2 tablespoons needed)
2 packages washed, ready-to-eat lettuce (16 cups needed)
5 lemons
2 limes (2 tablespoons needed)
1 pound green beans
1 pound snow peas
3 Haas avocados (3 cups needed)
1 bunch scallions (8 scallions needed)
4 medium tomatoes
1 package cherry tomatoes (2 cups needed)
3 cucumbers (5 cups cubed needed)
1 jalapeño pepper
1 red bell pepper (2 cups needed)

STAPLES

Balsamic vinegar
Canola oil
Olive oil
Olive oil spray
Garlic cloves
Minced garlic
Corn starch
Reduced-fat oil and vinegar dressing (see *Shop Smart*, opposite)
Salt
Black peppercorns

SUNDAY NIGHT

VEAL MEAT LOAF WITH ORANGE BARLEY

SERVES: 4
SERVING SIZE: 3 1/2 ounces ground veal, 1 cup vegetables, 2 tablespoons bread crumbs, 3/4 cup barley, 1 1/2 teaspoons oil
PREP TIME: 20 minutes
COOKING TIME: 30 minutes

Ground veal gives this meat loaf a light texture. The meat loaf bakes on a baking sheet rather than a loaf pan; the air circulates around the meat loaf speeding up the baking time.

HELPFUL HINTS:

- Vegetables can be chopped in a food processor.
- Make sure the oven is at temperature when you add the meat loaf.

COUNTDOWN:

- Preheat oven to 400°F.
- Prepare all ingredients.
- Make meat loaf.
- While meat loaf bakes, make barley.

VEAL MEAT LOAF

2 teaspoons olive oil
1 cup diced onion
1/2 cup diced celery
1/2 cup diced carrots
2 cups diced button mushrooms
1 pound lean ground veal*
1 cup chopped parsley
1/2 cup whole-wheat bread crumbs
1/2 teaspoon ground nutmeg
1/4 teaspoon salt
1/2 teaspoon freshly ground black pepper

1. Preheat oven to 400°F.

2. Heat oil in a nonstick skillet over medium-high heat. Add the onion and sauté 3 minutes. Add the celery, carrots, and mushrooms. Sauté for 5 minutes or until all liquid from the mushrooms is evaporated. Remove vegetables from heat.

3. In a large bowl, combine the ground veal and cooked vegetables. Add the parsley, bread crumbs, nutmeg, salt, and pepper. Mix well making sure all ingredients are combined.

4. Line a baking sheet with foil. Divide veal mixture into 4 parts on the sheet and mold into 4 small loaves, about 6 inches long and 3 inches wide each. Place in the oven for 15–20 minutes, or until the loaves are slightly pink in the middle. Serve with the Orange Barley.

**Look for lean ground veal containing per ounce: 43 calories, 2 g fat, 1 g saturated fat.*

ORANGE BARLEY

2 cups fat-free, no-salt-added chicken broth
1 cup quick-cooking pearl barley
4 teaspoons olive oil
2 tablespoons orange juice
1/4 teaspoon salt
1/4 teaspoon freshly ground black pepper

1. Bring broth to a boil in medium-size saucepan and add barley. Reduce heat to medium-high and simmer 10 minutes, uncovered.

2. Drain barley and add oil, orange juice, and salt and pepper.

COST OF MEAL PER PERSON

$2.64

PER SERVING

CHOICES/EXCHANGES
2 starch, 1 nonstarchy vegetable, 3 lean protein, 2 fat

Total Calories 490
Total Fat 16 g
Saturated Fat 5.3 g
Monounsaturated Fat 6.4 g
Trans Fat 0.0 g
Cholesterol 90 mg
Sodium 525 mg
Potassium 675 mg
Total Carbohydrate 53 g
Fiber 11 g
Sugars 5 g
Protein 32 g
Phosphorus 265 mg

MONDAY NIGHT

BUFFALO CHICKEN LEGS WITH BLUE CHEESE SALAD

SERVES: 4

SERVING SIZE: 5 ounces dark meat chicken, 3 tablespoons sauce, 1 1/2 teaspoons oil, 2 1/2 cups salad, 2 tablespoons dressing, 1/2 cup croutons

PREP TIME: 10 minutes

COOKING TIME: 20 minutes

With these Buffalo Chicken Legs, the heat level is up to you. I added a tangy, cool salad topped with blue cheese dressing to balance out the heat of the chicken.

HELPFUL HINTS:

- The chicken legs should be placed in one layer in the skillet. Use 2 skillets if needed.

COUNTDOWN:

- Prepare chicken ingredients.
- Make chicken.
- While chicken cooks, make salad.

BUFFALO CHICKEN LEGS

1 teaspoon cayenne pepper (2 teaspoons if you like it really hot)
6 tablespoons honey
8 tablespoons distilled white vinegar
8 tablespoons tomato paste
8 medium cloves garlic, crushed
4 tablespoons canola oil
6 pounds skinless chicken drumsticks with bone (half saved for Wednesday night)

1. In a medium bowl mix cayenne, honey, vinegar, tomato paste, and garlic together to form a smooth sauce. Set aside.

2. Heat oil in a large nonstick skillet over medium-high heat. Add the chicken in one layer and brown for 5 minutes, turn and brown 5 more minutes.

3. Reduce heat to low and add the sauce to the skillet, stir to coat chicken. Cover skillet and cook 5 minutes. A meat thermometer inserted into chicken should read 170°F.

4. Remove half the chicken, wrap, and store in the refrigerator for Wednesday night's dinner. Serve the remaining chicken on 4 dinner plates, scraping up sauce in pan to spoon over the chicken.

BLUE CHEESE SALAD

8 cups washed, ready-to-eat lettuce
2 cups sliced celery
2 cups whole-wheat croutons (about 4 ounces)
8 tablespoons low-calorie blue cheese dressing

1. Divide lettuce among 4 dinner plates. Add celery and croutons and drizzle with blue cheese dressing.

COST OF MEAL PER PERSON
$2.45

PER SERVING

CHOICES/EXCHANGES
1 starch, 1 carbohydrate, 1 nonstarchy vegetable, 5 lean protein, 1 1/2 fat

Total Calories 460
Total Fat 18 g
Saturated Fat 3.5 g
Monounsaturated Fat 7.3 g
Trans Fat 0.0 g
Cholesterol 140 mg
Sodium 550 mg
Potassium 1020 mg
Total Carbohydrate 35 g
Fiber 6 g
Sugars 19 g
Protein 40 g
Phosphorus 430 mg

TUESDAY NIGHT

LEMON PEPPER SCALLOPS AND COUSCOUS WITH GREEN BEANS AND HERBED GOAT CHEESE

SERVES: 4
SERVING SIZE: 5 ounces scallops,
1 cup green beans, 3/4 cup couscous,
1 tablespoon goat cheese, 1 teaspoon oil,
2 tablespoons basil
PREP TIME: 10 minutes
COOKING TIME: 20 minutes

Lemon juice and cracked black pepper give a spicy and tangy flavor to scallops. Herbed goat cheese, green beans, fresh basil, and couscous make an incredible and easy side dish to complete this simple dinner.

HELPFUL HINTS:

- Frozen scallops are a good choice for this recipe. Choose ones that are wild caught and flash frozen.
- Lemon juice is used in both the scallop and the couscous recipes. Measure out the lemon juice one time and divide accordingly.
- A quick way to chop basil is to wash and dry it and snip the leaves with a scissors.

COUNTDOWN:

- Marinate the scallops.
- Make couscous dish.
- Finish scallops.

LEMON PEPPER SCALLOPS

4 tablespoons fresh lemon juice
6 teaspoons olive oil, divided
1 teaspoon cracked black pepper
1 1/2 pounds frozen sea scallops (wild caught), defrosted

1. Mix lemon juice, 3 teaspoons olive oil, and cracked black pepper together in a small bowl.

2. Add scallops, toss a few times to make sure the scallops are coated with marinade, and marinate 5 minutes. Remove from marinade and drain.

3. Heat remaining 3 teaspoons olive oil in a nonstick skillet over high heat. When oil is smoking, add scallops and sauté on high 2 minutes. Turn and sauté 1 minute. Serve over the couscous.

COUSCOUS WITH GREEN BEANS AND HERBED GOAT CHEESE

2 cups water
1 pound green beans, cut into 1-inch pieces
1 cup precooked whole-grain couscous
4 tablespoons herbed goat cheese (1 ounce)
4 teaspoons olive oil
4 teaspoons lemon juice
1/4 teaspoon salt
1/4 teaspoon freshly ground black pepper
1/2 cup chopped fresh basil

1. Add water and green beans to a saucepan. Bring to a boil over high heat and boil 3 minutes.

2. Remove from heat, stir in couscous, and cover with a lid. Let stand 5 minutes.

3. Stir in goat cheese, oil, lemon juice, and salt and pepper.

4. To serve, place on individual dinner plates and add scallops on top. Sprinkle basil on top.

COST OF MEAL PER PERSON
$7.60

PER SERVING

CHOICES/EXCHANGES
2 starch, 1/2 carbohydrate, 2 nonstarchy vegetable, 4 lean protein, 1 1/2 fat

Total Calories 490
Total Fat 17 g
Saturated Fat 3.9 g
Monounsaturated Fat 6.5 g
Trans Fat 0.0 g
Cholesterol 60 mg
Sodium 500 mg
Potassium 370 mg
Total Carbohydrate 48 g
Fiber 6 g
Sugars 5 g
Protein 38 g
Phosphorus 175 mg

WEDNESDAY NIGHT

PANZANELLA SALAD (TUSCAN TOMATO AND BREAD SALAD)

SERVES: 4
SERVING SIZE: 5 ounces dark meat chicken,
1 1/2 slices whole-grain bread,
2 cups vegetables,
1 1/2 tablespoons dressing,
2 tablespoons pine nuts
PREP TIME: 15 minutes
COOKING TIME: 10 minutes

Fresh tomatoes, cucumbers, basil, olives, and 2-day-old bread are the basis for this Panzanella Salad. Adding the cooked chicken from Monday night to this salad turns it into a light and refreshing dinner.

HELPFUL HINTS:

- Any type of firm, country-style bread can be used. If it is too fresh, toast if for several minutes before using.
- Any type of reduced-fat salad dressing can be used.

COUNTDOWN:

- Prepare the salad ingredients.
- Soak bread.
- Make salad.
- Add the dressing.

PANZANELLA SALAD (TUSCAN TOMATO AND BREAD SALAD)

6 large slices whole-grain bread (1–2 days old)
8 scallions, sliced
4 medium tomatoes, cut into cubes (about 4 cups)
2 packed cups fresh basil leaves, torn into bite-size pieces
1 medium cucumber, peeled and cut into cubes (about 1 cup)
10 pitted black olives, cut in half
6 tablespoons reduced-fat oil and vinegar dressing, divided*
1 1/2 pounds chicken (saved from Monday night), cut off the bone into bite-size pieces
1/2 cup pine nuts

1. Soak the bread in a small bowl of water for a few seconds. When just soft, squeeze out all of the water and break bread into small pieces.

2. Place bread pieces in a bowl with the scallions, tomatoes, basil, cucumber, and olives. Add 4 tablespoons salad dressing and mix well. Divide among 4 dinner plates.

3. Add the chicken pieces to the plated salad. Sprinkle with pine nuts. Drizzle the 2 remaining tablespoons dressing over the salad.

**Look for reduced-fat oil and vinegar dressing containing per tablespoon: 11 calories, 1.0 g fat, 4 mg sodium.*

COST OF MEAL
PER PERSON
$4.79

PER SERVING

CHOICES/EXCHANGES
2 starch, 3 nonstarchy vegetable,
5 lean protein, 1 1/2 fat

Total Calories 520
Total Fat 18 g
Saturated Fat 3.1 g
Monounsaturated Fat 8.5 g
Trans Fat 0.0 g
Cholesterol 140 mg
Sodium 410 mg
Potassium 1275 mg
Total Carbohydrate 46 g
Fiber 7 g
Sugars 24 g
Protein 43 g
Phosphorus 455 mg

THURSDAY NIGHT

QUICK-FRIED DICED VEAL WITH SIMPLE FRIED RICE

SERVES: 4
SERVING SIZE: 5 ounces veal, 1/4 cup sauce, 1 3/4 cups snow peas, 3/4 cup rice
PREP TIME: 15 minutes
COOKING TIME: 15 minutes

Stir-fried veal and snow peas is a Chinese dinner that can be made at home faster than sending for Chinese takeout. It takes several minutes to gather and prepare the ingredients for stir-fried dishes, but only a few minutes to cook. One tip for a successful stir-fry is to line up all of the ingredients on a plate or cutting board in order of use. Substitute fat-free, no-salt-added chicken broth for sherry, if desired.

HELPFUL HINTS:

- Boneless, skinless chicken breasts can be substituted for the veal.
- 8 crushed garlic cloves can be used instead of bottled minced garlic.
- Your wok or skillet should be very hot so the veal will be crisp.

COUNTDOWN:

- Marinate veal.
- Prepare other ingredients.
- Microwave rice.
- Stir-fry veal dish.
- Stir-fry rice.

QUICK-FRIED DICED VEAL

1/2 cup sherry
4 tablespoons reduced-sodium soy sauce
4 teaspoons minced garlic
1 1/2 pounds veal cutlets
2 tablespoons cornstarch
3 tablespoons sesame oil, divided
1 pound snow peas
4 cups peeled cucumber cubes

1. In a small bowl, mix sherry, soy sauce, and garlic together. Cut veal into 1-inch pieces and add to marinade. Set aside while preparing remaining ingredients.

2. Remove veal from marinade, reserving marinade. Toss veal pieces in cornstarch and set aside. Heat 1 tablespoon sesame oil in a wok or skillet over high heat. Add snow peas and stir-fry 2 minutes. Remove snow peas to a plate.

3. Add remaining 2 tablespoons oil to the wok and then the veal. Stir-fry veal for 1 minute, then return the snow peas to the wok. Add the marinade, and cucumber. Stir-fry for 2 minutes.

4. Remove completed dish to a plate. Use the same wok to cook the rice dish.

SIMPLE FRIED RICE

Microwaveable brown rice (to make 3 cups cooked rice)
2 tablespoons sesame oil
1/2 teaspoon freshly ground black pepper

1. Cook rice according to package instructions. Measure 3 cups rice and reserve any remaining rice for another meal.

2. Add the sesame oil to the wok used to cook the veal and heat over high heat. Add the rice. Stir-fry 2 minutes. Sprinkle with pepper.

3. Divide among 4 dinner plates and serve veal and sauce on top.

COST OF MEAL PER PERSON

$8.37

PER SERVING

CHOICES/EXCHANGES
2 starch, 1/2 carbohydrate, 4 nonstarchy vegetable, 5 lean protein, 2 1/2 fat

Total Calories 650
Total Fat 22 g
Saturated Fat 3.8 g
Monounsaturated Fat 8.2 g
Trans Fat 0.0 g
Cholesterol 130 mg
Sodium 640 mg
Potassium 1255 mg
Total Carbohydrate 60 g
Fiber 7 g
Sugars 7 g
Protein 46 g
Phosphorus 655 mg

FRIDAY NIGHT

MEXICAN FIESTA BOWL

SERVES: 4
SERVING SIZE: 4 cups salad, 1/4 cup rice, 2 tablespoons dressing, 1 1/2 teaspoons almonds
PREP TIME: 15 minutes
COOKING TIME: 10 minutes

This dinner in a bowl is healthy, and quick and easy to make. This bowl features avocado, black beans, corn, tomato, and brown rice. You'll love this beautiful and delicious meal!

Avocado lends a nutty flavor and creamy texture to the bowl. Look for an avocado that gives slightly to pressure. To ripen an avocado, place it in a brown paper bag in a warm spot in your kitchen. Adding a banana or apple to the bag helps speed ripening. Only refrigerate avocados after they are ripe. They will keep for 2–3 days that way.

HELPFUL HINTS:

- Regular tomatoes cut into cubes can be used instead of cherry tomatoes.
- Any type of avocado can be used in this recipe.
- Place frozen corn in a colander and run under warm water to quickly defrost the kernels.

COUNTDOWN:

- Prepare each ingredient.
- Divide the ingredients into 4 portions and assemble them in 4 bowls.

MEXICAN FIESTA BOWL

3 Haas avocados, peeled, seeded, cut into 2-inch pieces (3 cups)
2 tablespoons lime juice
Microwaveable brown rice (to make 1 cup cooked rice)
8 cups washed, ready-to-eat lettuce
1 cup frozen corn kernels, defrosted
2 cups canned, rinsed, and drained low-sodium black beans
2 cups cherry tomatoes, cut in half
1/2 teaspoon salt
1 medium jalapeño, seeded and chopped
1/2 cup reduced-fat oil and vinegar dressing*
2 tablespoons sliced almonds
1/2 cup chopped cilantro

**Look for reduced-fat oil and vinegar dressing containing per tablespoon: 11 calories, 1.0 g fat, 4 mg sodium.*

1. Place avocado pieces in a bowl and toss with the lime juice.

2. Cook microwaveable rice according to package instructions and measure 1 cup. Reserve any remaining rice for another meal.

3. Divide lettuce among 4 large bowls. Spoon corn on one side of the lettuce, the black beans on another side, the tomatoes on a third side, and the rice on a fourth side. Place the avocado in the center. Sprinkle salt over tomatoes and avocado.

4. Mix the jalapeño pepper and dressing together in a small bowl and drizzle over the corn, black beans, and tomatoes. Sprinkle the almonds and cilantro on top.

COST OF MEAL PER PERSON

$2.90

PER SERVING

CHOICES/EXCHANGES
2 1/2 starch, 1/2 fruit,
1/2 carbohydrate,
2 nonstarchy vegetable,
1 lean protein, 3 fat

Total Calories 480
Total Fat 22 g
Saturated Fat 3.1 g
Monounsaturated Fat 14.2g
Trans Fat 0.0 g
Cholesterol 0 mg
Sodium 420 mg
Potassium 1635 mg
Total Carbohydrate 60 g
Fiber 21 g
Sugars 8 g
Protein 16 g
Phosphorus 405 mg

SATURDAY NIGHT

PAN-SEARED SCALLOPS WITH VEGETABLE MEDLEY RICE

SERVES: 4
SERVING SIZE: 5 ounces scallops, 1 1/2 teaspoons oil, 1 1/2 teaspoons chives, 3/4 cup rice, 1 cup vegetables, 2 1/2 tablespoons dressing
PREP TIME: 15 minutes
COOKING TIME: 15 minutes

Frozen sea scallops served with a colorful Vegetable Rice Medley make a quick dinner. Scallops, which need very little cooking, should be prepared so that the inside remains creamy. Prolonged cooking will shrink and toughen them.

The secret to searing the scallops is to make sure your skillet is very hot. If your scallops seem very large, check for doneness after searing by slicing into one. If the meat is opaque, they are done; if it is translucent cook them another 30 seconds.

HELPFUL HINTS:

- Freeze-dried chives can be substituted for fresh.
- 4 crushed garlic cloves can be used instead of bottled minced garlic.
- Sauté the vegetables in a skillet and, after removing the vegetables, use the same skillet to cook the scallops.

COUNTDOWN:

- Make rice dish.
- Sauté scallops.

PAN-SEARED SCALLOPS

2 tablespoons olive oil
1 1/2 pounds frozen sea scallops (wild caught), defrosted
2 tablespoons chopped chives
1/4 teaspoon salt
1/4 teaspoon freshly ground black pepper

1. Heat oil over high heat in the same nonstick skillet used to cook the vegetables. When oil is smoking, add scallops in one layer and sauté on high 2 minutes. Turn and sauté 1 more minute.

2. Remove to 4 dinner plates and sprinkle chives, salt, and pepper over scallops.

VEGETABLE MEDLEY RICE

Olive oil spray
1 cup diced onion
2 teaspoons minced garlic
2 cups diced red bell pepper
1 cup sliced button mushrooms
Microwaveable brown rice (to make 3 cups cooked rice)
1/2 cup reduced-fat sour cream
2 tablespoons prepared horseradish
1/4 teaspoon salt
1/4 teaspoon freshly ground black pepper

1. Heat a large nonstick skillet over medium-high heat and spray with olive oil spray.

2. Add onion and sauté until transparent, about 3 minutes. Add garlic, red pepper, and mushrooms. Continue to sauté about 3 more minutes. Remove vegetables to a serving bowl.

3. Make rice in the microwave according to package instructions. Measure 3 cups and add to the serving bowl. Reserve any remaining rice for another meal.

4. Mix sour cream and horseradish together in a small bowl. Mix sour cream mixture into the rice and add the salt and pepper.

COST OF MEAL PER PERSON
$9.23

PER SERVING

CHOICES/EXCHANGES
2 starch, 1 carbohydrate, 2 nonstarchy vegetable, 4 lean protein, 1 fat

Total Calories 490
Total Fat 15 g
Saturated Fat 3.9 g
Monounsaturated Fat 5.6 g
Trans Fat 0.0 g
Cholesterol 65 mg
Sodium 640 mg
Potassium 465 mg
Total Carbohydrate 54 g
Fiber 5 g
Sugars 5 g
Protein 36 g
Phosphorus 240 mg

WEEK **ELEVEN**

WEEKLY BUDGET
Average cost of a meal per person for the week is
$5.31

SUNDAY NIGHT
GARLIC STEAK AND LINGUINE WITH SHREDDED CARROTS

Garlic and parsley smother this pan-sautéed steak. The garlic is blanched first to give it a mild, sweet flavor.

MONDAY NIGHT
SEARED TUNA WITH CAULIFLOWER MASHED "POTATOES"

These tuna steaks are seared in minutes to create a crusty exterior and a tender, juicy interior. Savor the "mashed potatoes" made with cauliflower instead of potatoes. Wild mushrooms give the mash an earthy flavor.

TUESDAY NIGHT
CHICKEN TIKKA MASALA WITH CARAWAY RICE

This is a delicately spiced Indian chicken. It captures the flavors of India without taking hours to prepare. Garam masala, found in the spice section of the supermarket, is the secret to this dish. It's added at the end of the cooking so it retains its aroma.

WEDNESDAY NIGHT
TUNA MELT WITH SAUTÉED GREEN BEANS

Enjoy this tuna patty with melted cheese on top for a tasty midweek dinner. Keep frozen green beans on hand for a quick side dish.

THURSDAY NIGHT
HOT AND SPICY STIR-FRY BEEF WITH SESAME NOODLES

Pacific Rim flavors such as ginger, sesame oil and seeds, and peanuts make a tasty dinner. Fresh ginger is the secret to this dish.

FRIDAY NIGHT
PAN-GRILLED QUESADILLAS WITH SPINACH SALAD

A savory bean mixture and melted cheese fill tortillas to create an earthy, Southwestern vegetarian dinner. A fresh spinach salad sprinkled with pecans completes the meal.

SATURDAY NIGHT
CAJUN CHICKEN WITH RICE AND RED BEANS

Hot Cajun spices contrast with sweet grapes in this Louisiana-inspired dinner. To make you feel like you are on the Bayou, the dinner is completed with traditional red beans and rice.

SHOPPING LIST

Here is the Shopping List for this week's dinners.

This shopping list will help you get in and out of the market quickly. The ingredients are listed by supermarket department to make shopping easier; you won't forget something in one department and have to go back and forth across the store.

The amount needed of each ingredient is listed so you will know what size package or can to buy. If it helps you to better visualize the amount you need, please note that 4 tablespoons equal 1/4 cup and 8 tablespoons equal 1/2 cup.

Make sure to check your refrigerator and pantry to see if you have any of these ingredients on hand before making your trip to the market.

MEAT AND SEAFOOD

3 pounds boneless, skinless chicken thighs
1 1/2 pounds fresh tuna steaks
3 pounds grass-fed strip steak

DAIRY

1 small carton light cream (4 tablespoons needed)
1 bottle skim milk (3/4 cup needed)
1 carton reduced-fat sour cream (3/4 cup needed)
1 package shredded, reduced-fat Swiss cheese (1 cup needed)
1 package shredded, reduced-fat Monterey Jack cheese (3/4 cup needed)
1 small piece Parmesan cheese (4 tablespoons needed)

BAKERY

1 container whole-wheat bread crumbs (1/2 cup needed)
1 loaf whole-wheat or multigrain bread (8 slices needed)
1 package 8-inch whole-wheat tortillas (8 tortillas needed)

SHOP SMART

- Look for a salt-free or low-sodium Cajun seasoning blend. McCormick Perfect Pinch Cajun Seasoning or The Spice Hunter salt-free Cajun Seasoning blend fit this profile. It is important to make sure it's salt-free or low-sodium.
- Look for reduced-fat oil and vinegar dressing containing per tablespoon: 11 calories, 1.0 g fat, 4 mg sodium.

CONDIMENTS

1 small bottle low-fat mayonnaise (4 tablespoons needed)
1 small bottle hot pepper sauce
1 small bottle sesame oil (3 1/2 tablespoons needed)
1 small bottle balsamic vinegar (2 tablespoons needed)

SPICES AND SEEDS

1 small bottle ground ginger (2 teaspoons needed)
1 small bottle ground coriander (4 teaspoons needed)
1 small bottle ground turmeric (1 teaspoon needed)
1 small bottle garam masala (4 teaspoons needed)
1 small bottle caraway seeds (2 tablespoons needed)
1 small package sesame seeds (4 tablespoons needed)
1 small bottle salt-free or low-sodium Cajun seasoning (2 tablespoons needed) (see *Shop Smart*, opposite)

CANNED FOODS AND FROZEN FOODS

Canned tuna packed in water (20 ounces needed)
1 package frozen sliced green beans (1 pound needed)
1 small can tomato paste (1/2 cup needed)
1 small package frozen peas (1 cup needed)
1 can low-sodium, small red kidney beans (1 cup needed)
1 can navy beans (1 1/2 cups needed)
1 package frozen chopped green bell pepper (2 cups needed)
1 container sliced red pimentos (1 cup needed)
1 container fat-free, no-salt-added chicken broth (1 1/2 cups needed)

RICE, PASTA, BARLEY, COUSCOUS

Microwaveable brown rice (to make 5 1/2 cups cooked rice)
1/2 pound fresh or dried whole-wheat linguine
1/2 pound steamed or fresh Chinese noodles

NUTS

1 small jar dry-roasted, unsalted peanuts (4 tablespoons needed)
1 package pecan halves (1 1/2 cups needed)

PRODUCE

3 onions (3 cups needed)
1 red onion (8 tablespoons needed)
6 tomatoes (16 slices and 4 cups diced needed)
1 bunch cilantro (3/4 cup needed)
1 bunch parsley (1 cup plus 2 tablespoons needed)
1 bunch chives (1/2 cup needed)
1 container shiitake mushrooms (4 cups needed)
1 head cauliflower (8 cups needed)
2 lemons
1 package shredded carrots (4 cups needed)
1 small piece fresh ginger (4 tablespoons needed)
1/4 pound red seedless grapes
1/4 pound green seedless grapes
3 medium jalapeño peppers
1 bag washed, ready-to-eat spinach (4 cups needed)

STAPLES

Canola oil
Olive oil
Olive oil spray
Garlic (18 cloves needed)
Minced garlic
Reduced-fat oil and vinegar dressing (see *Shop Smart*, opposite)
Salt
Black peppercorns

SUNDAY NIGHT

GARLIC STEAK AND LINGUINE WITH SHREDDED CARROTS

SERVES: 4
SERVING SIZE: 5 ounces steak, 1/4 cup garlic–parsley topping, 3/4 cup linguine, 1 cup carrots, 1 tablespoon cheese
PREP TIME: 15 minutes
COOKING TIME: 30 minutes

This juicy steak is smothered in garlic and parsley. The garlic cloves are blanched first and then chopped with fresh parsley. Blanching gives the garlic a mild, sweet flavor. The water used for blanching the garlic has a wonderful flavor so I add it to the water used to cook the pasta.

Half of the steak cooked for this meal is saved for Thursday night's dinner.

HELPFUL HINTS:

- Use the same pot for boiling the garlic and the pasta to save cleaning up time.
- The blanched garlic and parsley can be chopped in a food processor.

COUNTDOWN:

- Blanch garlic and then fill the pot with more water and place over high heat to boil.
- Make steak.
- Make pasta and carrots.

GARLIC STEAK

3 pounds grass-fed strip steak (about 3/4 inch thick), visible fat removed
12 cloves garlic, peeled
3/4 cup chopped parsley
1/4 teaspoon salt
1/2 teaspoon freshly ground black pepper
2 teaspoons olive oil

1. Remove visible fat from steak.

2. Place whole, peeled garlic cloves in a large saucepan and cover with cold water. Bring to a boil and scoop out garlic cloves with a strainer. Add more water and use same saucepan to cook pasta for side dish.

3. Chop the garlic and parsley together (you can use a food processor if desired). Add salt and pepper. Set aside.

4. Heat a large nonstick skillet over medium-high heat and add the steak. Sauté 5 minutes. Turn and sauté 5 more minutes. A meat thermometer inserted into steak should read 135°F for medium rare. Cook 2–3 minutes longer if you prefer it more well done.

5. Remove steak from skillet to a cutting board and add the olive oil to the skillet. Add garlic and parsley mixture to the skillet and sauté 2–3 minutes.

6. Remove half the steak from the cutting board and refrigerate it for Thursday night's dinner. Cut the remaining steak into 1-inch slices and divide among 4 dinner plates. Spoon sautéed garlic and parsley mixture on top of slices.

LINGUINE WITH SHREDDED CARROTS

1/2 pound fresh or dried whole-wheat linguine
4 cups shredded carrots
2 tablespoons olive oil
1/4 teaspoon salt
1/2 teaspoon freshly ground black pepper
4 tablespoons freshly grated Parmesan cheese

1. Fill the saucepan used for blanching the garlic with 3–4 quarts water and bring to a boil. Add the pasta and boil 3 minutes for fresh pasta, 8 minutes for dried.

2. Add the carrots to the water just to warm. Remove 1/4 cup of the water to a large bowl and drain pasta and carrots.

3. Add olive oil and salt and pepper to the bowl. Add the drained pasta and carrots and toss well. Divide among 4 dinner plates and sprinkle with Parmesan cheese.

COST OF MEAL
PER PERSON
$8.23

PER SERVING

CHOICES/EXCHANGES
2 1/2 starch, 1/2 carbohydrate,
2 nonstarchy vegetable,
6 lean protein, 1/2 fat

Total Calories 560
Total Fat 17 g
Saturated Fat 4.1 g
Monounsaturated Fat 6.6 g
Trans Fat 0.0 g
Cholesterol 100 mg
Sodium 570 mg
Potassium 1295 mg
Total Carbohydrate 57 g
Fiber 9 g
Sugars 7 g
Protein 51 g
Phosphorus 645 mg

MONDAY NIGHT

SEARED TUNA WITH CAULIFLOWER MASHED "POTATOES"

SERVES: 4
SERVING SIZE: 5 ounces tuna,
1 tablespoon parsley,
3 1/2 cups cauliflower and mushroom mash
PREP TIME: 15 minutes
COOKING TIME: 30 minutes

Fresh tuna takes only minutes to make. The secret is to have a very hot skillet so that the tuna sears on each side, leaving the center rare.

Cauliflower is microwaved and mashed to look like mashed potatoes for the side dish. Wild mushrooms are added to give the side dish an earthy flavor.

HELPFUL HINTS:

- Minced garlic can be found in the produce section of the market.
- A quick way to chop chives is to snip them with a scissors.
- Use the same skillet for the tuna and mushrooms. Sauté the mushrooms first and remove before cooking the tuna.

COUNTDOWN:

- Sauté mushrooms and garlic.
- Make cauliflower.
- Sear tuna.

SEARED TUNA

2 teaspoons canola oil
1 1/2 pounds fresh tuna steaks
1/4 teaspoon salt
1/2 teaspoon freshly ground black pepper
4 tablespoons chopped fresh parsley

1. In the same large nonstick skillet used to cook the mushrooms, heat oil over high heat.

2. Add tuna and sear for 1 minute. Turn and sprinkle salt and pepper on the cooked side. Sear second side for 1 minute for a 1/2-inch-thick tuna steak. (For a 1-inch-thick tuna steak, lower heat and cook 2 more minutes. If you like your tuna more well done, increase the cooking time.)

3. Remove to a cutting board, slice, and divide among 4 dinner plates. Sprinkle parsley on top.

CAULIFLOWER MASHED "POTATOES"

1/2 cup whole-wheat bread crumbs
4 teaspoons canola oil
4 cups sliced shiitake mushrooms
4 teaspoons minced garlic
1 head cauliflower (8 cups florets and stems)
3/4 cup skim milk
3/4 cup reduced-fat sour cream
1/2 cup chopped chives
14 teaspoon salt
1/2 teaspoon freshly ground black pepper

1. Place bread crumbs on a foil-lined sheet and toast in a toaster oven or under the broiler for 2–3 minutes. Watch to make sure they don't burn. Set aside.

2. Heat canola oil in a large nonstick skillet over medium-high heat and sauté the mushrooms for 3 minutes. Add the garlic and continue to sauté 1 minute. Remove mushrooms and garlic from skillet to a bowl and sprinkle bread crumbs on top. Set aside. Use the same skillet to sear the tuna.

3. Separate the cauliflower into florets and coarsely chop the core. Place cauliflower in a microwave-safe bowl and microwave on high 8 minutes. Test to see if the cauliflower is soft. (Microwave another 2 minutes, if needed.)

4. Chop the cauliflower in a food processor or by hand. Add the skim milk and sour cream and continue to process until smooth.

5. Transfer mash to the bowl with the mushrooms mixture and stir in the chives, salt, and pepper.

COST OF MEAL PER PERSON

$5.92

PER SERVING

CHOICES/EXCHANGES
1/2 starch, 1/2 fat-free milk, 3 nonstarchy vegetable, 5 lean protein, 1 fat

Total Calories 430
Total Fat 15 g
Saturated Fat 4.7 g
Monounsaturated Fat 6.3 g
Trans Fat 0.0 g
Cholesterol 95 mg
Sodium 510 mg
Potassium 1095 mg
Total Carbohydrate 25 g
Fiber 6 g
Sugars 9 g
Protein 51 g
Phosphorus 285 mg

TUESDAY NIGHT

CHICKEN TIKKA MASALA WITH CARAWAY RICE

SERVES: 4

SERVING SIZE: 5 ounces dark meat chicken, 2 teaspoons oil, 1 1/4 cups vegetables, 1 tablespoon light cream, 3/4 cup rice, 1 1/2 teaspoons caraway seeds, 4 teaspoons spices

PREP TIME: 20 minutes

COOKING TIME: 15 minutes

Delicately spiced Indian food usually takes time to make. But this is a quick version of an Indian classic capturing the flavors of this dish without hours spent to make it. Half the chicken is used for this dinner. The remaining half is used for Saturday night's dinner.

Spices are the secret to Indian cooking. It's worth gathering a few together for this dish. Garam masala is an important addition to the recipe. It's a combination of spices usually made with cardamom, cloves, cumin, cinnamon, black pepper, and nutmeg. Add it at the end of the cooking time so it retains its aroma. Garam masala is available in the spice section of the market. Try it over other foods such as vegetables or rice.

HELPFUL HINTS:

- Spices keep for about 6 months. Buy new ones if yours are older.

COUNTDOWN:

- Prepare all ingredients first.
- Start chicken.
- While chicken cooks, make rice.

CHICKEN TIKKA MASALA

4 teaspoons canola oil
1 1/2 pounds boneless, skinless chicken thighs, cut into 1/2-inch pieces
1 cup sliced onion
2 teaspoons ground ginger
4 teaspoons ground coriander
1 teaspoon ground turmeric
4 teaspoons minced garlic
4 cups diced tomato
1 1/2 cups fat-free, no-salt-added chicken broth
4 tablespoons light cream
4 teaspoons garam masala
4 tablespoons chopped cilantro
1/4 teaspoon salt

1. Heat oil in a large nonstick skillet over medium-high heat. Add chicken and onion. Sauté 2 minutes, turning the chicken to brown on all sides.

2. Add ginger, coriander, turmeric, and garlic. Sauté 1 minute.

3. Add tomato and broth and cook 5 minutes. Add cream and garam masala. Stir to combine and cook gently 3 minutes.

4. Sprinkle with cilantro and salt, and serve over the rice.

CARAWAY RICE

Microwaveable brown rice (to make 3 cups cooked rice)
4 teaspoons canola oil
2 tablespoons caraway seeds
1/4 teaspoon salt
1/2 teaspoon freshly ground black pepper

1. Microwave rice according to package instructions. Measure 3 cups rice and reserve any remaining rice for another meal.

2. Add oil, caraway seeds, and salt and pepper to the rice. Toss well and serve.

COST OF MEAL PER PERSON

$3.78

PER SERVING

CHOICES/EXCHANGES
2 starch, 1 carbohydrate, 2 nonstarchy vegetable, 5 lean protein, 2 fat

Total Calories 590
Total Fat 22 g
Saturated Fat 4.9 g
Monounsaturated Fat 9.7 g
Trans Fat 0.0 g
Cholesterol 150 mg
Sodium 520 mg
Potassium 1315 mg
Total Carbohydrate 55 g
Fiber 7 g
Sugars 7 g
Protein 44 g
Phosphorus 590 mg

WEDNESDAY NIGHT

TUNA MELT WITH SAUTÉED GREEN BEANS

SERVES: 4
SERVING SIZE: 5 ounces tuna,
1 1/2 cups vegetables,
1 tablespoon mayonnaise, 1/4 cup cheese,
2 slices whole-grain bread, 1 1/2 teaspoons oil,
4 tablespoons pecans
PREP TIME: 15 minutes
COOKING TIME: 20 minutes

Keep some canned tuna on hand for quick family dinners like this one. Also, keep some frozen green beans on hand for a fast and easy side dish. Frozen vegetables can be a good alternative to fresh; vegetables grown for freezing are picked at their peak and flash frozen, which allows them to retain much of their nutrient value.

HELPFUL HINTS:

- Any type of chopped onion can be used.

COUNTDOWN:

- Preheat broiler.
- Prepare tuna melt.
- Make beans.

TUNA MELT

3 3/4 cups canned tuna packed in water, drained (about 1 1/4 pounds)
4 tablespoons chopped red onion
4 tablespoons low-fat mayonnaise
2 tablespoons lemon juice
2 tablespoons chopped parsley
1/2 teaspoon freshly ground black pepper
8 slices whole-wheat or multigrain bread
16 tomato slices
1 cup shredded, reduced-fat Swiss cheese

1. Preheat broiler. Line a baking tray with foil and place in broiler while it heats.

2. Meanwhile, combine tuna, onion, mayonnaise, lemon juice, parsley, and pepper in a bowl.

3. Toast bread. Divide the tuna mixture evenly among the slices and spread over each slice. Place two tomato slices over the tuna on each slice of bread. Sprinkle the cheese on top.

4. Carefully put bread slices on the preheated baking tray and place under the broiler, about 10 inches from the heat until the cheese melts and is golden brown, about 3–4 minutes.

SAUTÉED GREEN BEANS

1 pound frozen sliced green beans, defrosted
2 tablespoons olive oil
1 cup pecans
1/2 teaspoon freshly ground black pepper

1. Place green beans in a colander in the sink. Run warm water over them to defrost, then drain well. Pat dry with paper towel.

2. Heat oil in a large nonstick skillet over medium-high heat. Add beans and sauté 4–5 minutes until they are warmed through.

3. Break pecans into small pieces and add to the skillet. Sauté another minute. Remove from heat, add pepper, and serve.

COST OF MEAL PER PERSON

$4.07

PER SERVING

CHOICES/EXCHANGES
2 starch, 2 nonstarchy vegetable, 5 lean protein, 5 1/2 fat

Total Calories 660
Total Fat 36 g
Saturated Fat 5.1 g
Monounsaturated Fat 16.3 g
Trans Fat 0.0 g
Cholesterol 60 mg
Sodium 650 mg
Potassium 1060 mg
Total Carbohydrate 43 g
Fiber 11 g
Sugars 12 g
Protein 45 g
Phosphorus 635 mg

THURSDAY NIGHT

HOT AND SPICY STIR-FRY BEEF WITH SESAME NOODLES

SERVES: 4

SERVING SIZE: 5 ounces steak, 3/4 cup vegetables, 1/4 cup sauce, 1 tablespoon peanuts, 3/4 cup Chinese noodles, 1 tablespoon sesame seeds, 3/4 tablespoon oil

PREP TIME: 15 minutes

COOKING TIME: 15 minutes

This dinner is a delicious mixture of Pacific Rim flavors! Fresh ginger is the secret to the exotic taste of this dish. A quick way to add fresh ginger to a dish is to grate it over the food.

HELPFUL HINTS:

- If using ground ginger instead of fresh, mix it in with the sauce.
- A quick way to defrost peas is to put them in a colander and run hot water over them.
- Angel hair pasta can be used if Chinese noodles are not available.
- Minced garlic can be found in the produce section of the market.

COUNTDOWN:

- Prepare all ingredients.
- Make noodles.
- Stir-fry beef dish.

HOT AND SPICY STIR-FRY BEEF

1/2 cup tomato paste
Several drops hot pepper sauce
1/2 cup water
1 1/2 tablespoons sesame oil
2 cups sliced onion
3 teaspoons minced garlic
4 tablespoons chopped fresh ginger OR 4 teaspoons ground ginger
1 1/4 pounds steak (saved from Sunday night), cut into 1/2-inch strips
4 tablespoons dry-roasted, unsalted peanuts

1. Mix tomato paste, hot pepper sauce, and water together and set aside.

2. Heat the oil in a large wok or skillet over high heat. Add the onion, garlic, and chopped ginger. Stir-fry 2 minutes.

3. Add steak to the skillet and stir-fry 2 minutes. Add tomato paste mixture and toss with the ingredients for a few seconds. Remove to a plate and sprinkle with peanuts.

SESAME NOODLES

1/2 pound steamed or fresh Chinese noodles
1 cup frozen peas, defrosted
2 tablespoons sesame oil
1/2 teaspoon salt
1/2 teaspoon freshly ground black pepper
4 tablespoons sesame seeds

1. Fill a large saucepan with water and bring it to a boil. Add noodles and cook for 1 minute. Add peas and continue to cook for 1 minute.

2. Drain noodles and peas. Toss with sesame oil and add salt and pepper. Remove to 4 dinner plates and sprinkle sesame seeds on top.

COST OF MEAL PER PERSON
$9.65

PER SERVING

CHOICES/EXCHANGES
3 starch, 2 nonstarchy vegetable, 6 lean protein, 3 fat

Total Calories 680
Total Fat 28 g
Saturated Fat 5.5 g
Monounsaturated Fat 11.2 g
Trans Fat 0.0 g
Cholesterol 145 mg
Sodium 410 mg
Potassium 1040 mg
Total Carbohydrate 56 g
Fiber 6 g
Sugars 6 g
Protein 53 g
Phosphorus 635 mg

FRIDAY NIGHT

PAN-GRILLED QUESADILLAS WITH SPINACH SALAD

SERVES: 4
SERVING SIZE: 1 1/2 cups vegetables, 1/3 cup beans, 2 whole-wheat tortillas, 3 tablespoons cheese, 2 tablespoons pecans, 1 tablespoon dressing
PREP TIME: 15 minutes
COOKING TIME: 20 minutes

Tortillas filled with a savory bean mixture and gooey melted cheese make an easy Southwestern dinner the whole family will love.

The side dish for this meal has a smoky chipotle dressing. Chipotle chili powder found in the spice section of the supermarket lends a smoked flavor to the bottled dressing. It can, also, be sprinkled on many other ingredients and makes a great sauce when mixed with mayonnaise.

HELPFUL HINTS:

- Any type of reduced-fat Mexican-style cheese can be used.
- Cannellini beans can be used instead of navy beans.
- Use two skillets to speed cooking time and avoid having to repeat the recipe.

COUNTDOWN:

- Assemble salad.
- Make quesadillas.

PAN-GRILLED QUESADILLAS

1 cup drained sliced red pimentos
6 medium cloves garlic
1/4 cup sliced red onion
1 1/2 cups rinsed and drained reduced-sodium navy beans
Several drops hot pepper sauce
1/4 teaspoon salt
1/2 teaspoon freshly ground black pepper
8 (8-inch) whole-wheat tortillas
3/4 cup shredded, reduced-fat Monterey Jack cheese
3 medium jalapeño peppers, seeded and chopped
1/2 cup fresh cilantro

1. Squeeze pimentos in paper towels to make sure they are well drained.

2. Chop garlic, onion, and pimentos in a food processor. Add the beans and hot pepper sauce to the food processor and purée. If mixing by hand, mash beans with a fork, chop pimentos, crush the garlic, dice the onion, and combine, adding hot pepper sauce. Add salt and pepper.

3. Spread bean mixture evenly among 4 tortillas. Sprinkle cheese, jalapeño peppers, and cilantro on top. Cover each with one of the 4 remaining tortillas.

4. Heat 2 large nonstick skillets over high heat. When hot, place 1 quesadilla in each pan. Cook for 1 minute, turn them over, cook 1 more minute, and remove to a cutting board. Repeat this step with the remaining tortillas.

5. Cut each tortilla into 4 wedges. Place 4 wedges on each plate and serve with the salad.

SPINACH SALAD

1/2 cup pecan halves
4 cups washed, ready-to-eat spinach
4 tablespoons reduced-fat oil and vinegar dressing*

1. Place pecans in a toaster oven or under a broiler to toast, about 2–3 minutes. Watch to make sure they do not burn.

2. Place spinach in a bowl and sprinkle pecans on top. Drizzle dressing over the salad.

**Look for reduced-fat oil and vinegar dressing containing per tablespoon: 11 calories, 1.0 g fat, 4 mg sodium.*

COST OF MEAL PER PERSON

$2.67

PER SERVING

CHOICES/EXCHANGES
3 1/2 starch, 1 nonstarchy vegetable, 1 lean protein, 3 fat

Total Calories 460
Total Fat 19 g
Saturated Fat 4.8 g
Monounsaturated Fat 7.0 g
Trans Fat 0.0 g
Cholesterol 15 mg
Sodium 570 mg
Potassium 790 mg
Total Carbohydrate 58 g
Fiber 12 g
Sugars 5 g
Protein 21 g
Phosphorus 480 mg

SATURDAY NIGHT

CAJUN CHICKEN WITH RICE AND RED BEANS

SERVES: 4
SERVING SIZE: 5 ounces dark meat chicken, 1 tablespoon oil, 1/4 cup grapes, 1/2 cup plus 2 tablespoons rice, 1/4 cup beans
PREP TIME: 15 minutes
COOKING TIME: 25 minutes

Hot Cajun spices are contrasted with sweet grapes in this chicken dish. Boneless, skinless chicken thighs are a flavorful alternative to chicken breasts. There are many Cajun spice blends to choose from. They normally include cayenne pepper, chili powder, onion powder, and garlic powder. I like the salt-free blends that are available in the supermarket.

HELPFUL HINTS:

- Cajun seasoning blends can be found in the spice section of the supermarket.
- A quick way to defrost frozen chopped green bell peppers is to place them in a colander and run hot water over them.

COUNTDOWN:

- Prepare ingredients for chicken and rice.
- Make rice.
- Make chicken.

CAJUN CHICKEN

6 teaspoons canola oil, divided
2 tablespoons balsamic vinegar
4 tablespoons water
1 1/2 pounds boneless, skinless chicken thighs
2 tablespoons Cajun seasoning*
1/2 teaspoon salt
1 1/4 cups mixed seedless red and green grapes, cut in half

1. Mix 4 teaspoons canola oil, balsamic vinegar, and water together and set aside.

2. Open chicken thighs flat. This can be done where the bone has been removed. Remove all visible fat. Sprinkle Cajun seasoning evenly over both sides of chicken.

3. Heat remaining 2 teaspoons canola oil in a large nonstick skillet over medium-high heat. Add chicken and sauté 3 minutes. Turn and sauté 3 minutes. Watch chicken to make sure spices do not burn. Lower heat if needed. A meat thermometer inserted into chicken should read 175°F. Remove to a plate and sprinkle with salt.

4. Add the oil and vinegar mixture and the grapes to the skillet. Cook over medium heat, scraping up the brown bits in the skillet, for 2 minutes or until sauce is warmed through. Serve over chicken.

** Look for a salt-free or low-sodium Cajun seasoning blend. McCormick Perfect Pinch Cajun Seasoning or The Spice Hunter salt-free Cajun Seasoning blend fit this profile. It is important to make sure it's salt-free or low-sodium.*

RICE AND RED BEANS

Microwaveable brown rice (to make 2 1/2 cups cooked rice)
1 cup canned, low-sodium, small red kidney beans, rinsed and drained
2 cups frozen chopped green bell pepper, defrosted
Several drops hot pepper sauce
2 tablespoons canola oil
1/4 teaspoon salt
1/2 teaspoon freshly ground black pepper

1. Microwave rice according to package instructions. Measure 2 1/2 cups rice and reserve any remaining rice for another time. Add rice to a bowl.

2. Rinse and drain beans and add to the bowl with green bell pepper. Add hot pepper sauce, canola oil, and salt and pepper. Toss well.

COST OF MEAL PER PERSON

$2.88

PER SERVING

CHOICES/EXCHANGES
2 1/2 starch, 1/2 fruit, 1/2 carbohydrate, 1 nonstarchy vegetable, 5 lean protein, 2 1/2 fat

Total Calories 620
Total Fat 23 g
Saturated Fat 3.4 g
Monounsaturated Fat 11.3 g
Trans Fat 0.0 g
Cholesterol 140 mg
Sodium 620 mg
Potassium 855 mg
Total Carbohydrate 59 g
Fiber 7 g
Sugars 12 g
Protein 44 g
Phosphorus 505 mg

WEEK **TWELVE**

WEEKLY BUDGET
Average cost of a meal per person for the week is
$4.52

SUNDAY NIGHT
PORK AND MUSHROOM SKILLET SUPPER

Smoked paprika gives a smoky flavor to juicy, tender pork. This is a one-pot meal with the pasta cooked right in the skillet with the other ingredients.

MONDAY NIGHT
SALMON BURGERS WITH SAUTÉED BROCCOLI RAAB

A mayonnaise and relish sauce adds flavor to these juicy burgers. Garlic-flavored broccoli raab completes the dinner.

TUESDAY NIGHT
GREEK GYRO SANDWICH WITH TZATZIKI SAUCE

These pita bread sandwiches are filled with sautéed pork, tomatoes, and lettuce. They're topped with a yogurt-based sauce flavored with cucumbers and spices.

WEDNESDAY NIGHT
SALMON CHOWDER

This is a family-pleasing chowder made with salmon, vegetables, fresh herbs, and a tangy mustard cream sauce. It's a one-pot meal.

THURSDAY NIGHT
TURKEY POT PIE

This easy pot pie has a golden crust made with refrigerated biscuit dough. It has a smoky flavor from the addition of smoked paprika.

FRIDAY NIGHT
RICOTTA SOUFFLÉ WITH TOMATO BRUSCHETTA

Ricotta cheese and vegetables are topped with bread crumbs in this unusual and easy-to-make soufflé.

SATURDAY NIGHT
TURKEY HASH

Cranberry sauce adds a sweet and tart flavor to turkey, vegetables, and sweet potatoes in this dinner. It's quick to make using reserved cooked turkey from Thursday night's dinner.

SHOPPING LIST

SHOP SMART

- Look for low-sodium, no-sugar-added pasta sauce containing per 1/2 cup: 112 calories, 3.5 g fat, 17.7 g carbohydrate, 39 mg sodium.
- Look for reduced-fat oil and vinegar dressing containing per tablespoon: 11 calories, 1.0 g fat, 4 mg sodium.

Here is the Shopping List for this week's dinners.

This shopping list will help you get in and out of the market quickly. The ingredients are listed by supermarket department to make shopping easier; you won't forget something in one department and have to go back and forth across the store.

The amount needed of each ingredient is listed so you will know what size package or can to buy. If it helps you to better visualize the amount you need, please note that 4 tablespoons equal 1/4 cup and 8 tablespoons equal 1/2 cup.

Make sure to check your refrigerator and pantry to see if you have any of these ingredients on hand before making your trip to the market.

MEAT AND SEAFOOD
3 pounds pork tenderloin
2 3/4 pounds salmon fillets (wild caught, skin removed)
3 pounds turkey tenderloin

DAIRY
1 carton eggs (4 needed)
1 carton plain, nonfat yogurt (1 cup needed)
1 carton whipping cream (1/4 cup needed)
1 carton nonfat ricotta cheese (2 cups needed)
1 small package shredded, reduced-fat Monterey Jack cheese (1 cup needed)

BAKERY
1 container plain whole-wheat bread crumbs (2 3/4 cups needed)
1 package 2-ounce whole-wheat hamburger rolls (4 rolls needed)
1 package 6-inch whole-wheat pita breads (4 needed)
1 small whole-wheat baguette (8, 3/4-ounce slices needed)
1 small package refrigerated biscuit dough (3, 2-ounce biscuits needed)

CONDIMENTS

1 small bottle low-sodium, no-sugar-added pasta sauce (1 1/2 cups needed) (see *Shop Smart*, opposite)
1 small bottle reduced-fat mayonnaise (4 tablespoons needed)
1 small bottle sweet pickle relish (3 tablespoons needed)
1 small jar Dijon mustard (2 tablespoons needed)
1 can sliced sweet pimentos (1 cup needed)
1 container whole berry cranberry sauce (1 1/3 cups needed)

SPICES AND NUTS

1 bottle smoked paprika (5 tablespoons needed)
1 bottle dried oregano (2 teaspoons needed)

CANNED FOODS AND FROZEN FOODS

1 large package frozen chopped onion (6 cups needed)
1 large package frozen chopped green bell pepper (7 cups needed)
1 package frozen peas (1 cup needed)
1 container fat-free, no-salt-added chicken broth (4 cups needed)

RICE, PASTA, BARLEY, COUSCOUS

6 ounces fresh angel hair pasta

ALCOHOL AND SPIRITS

1 bottle red wine (1 cup needed)

PRODUCE

5 tomatoes (5 cups needed)
4 onions (3 1/2 cups needed)
1 red onion (1 cup needed)
1 1/2 pounds sliced baby bello mushrooms (9 cups needed)
1/2 pound sliced button mushrooms (3 cups needed)
1/2 pound green beans (2 cups needed)
1 zucchini (2 cups needed)
2 lemons
1 package shredded lettuce (2 cups needed)
1 cucumber
1 bunch celery (3 cups needed)
1 package peeled carrots (3 cups needed)
2 pounds russet or Idaho potatoes
10 ounces sweet potatoes
1 pound broccoli raab
1 bunch cilantro (1cup needed)
1 bunch dill (1 tablespoon needed)
1 bunch fresh thyme (1/2 cup needed)
1 bunch fresh chives (1/2 cup needed)
1 bunch tarragon (3 tablespoons needed)
1 bunch basil (1 cup needed)

STAPLES

Canola oil
Olive oil
Olive oil spray
Garlic
Minced garlic
Flour
Reduced-fat oil and vinegar dressing (see *Shop Smart*, opposite)
Salt
Black peppercorns

SUNDAY NIGHT

PORK AND MUSHROOM SKILLET SUPPER

SERVES: 4

SERVING SIZE: 5 ounces pork, 3/4 teaspoon oil, 3 cups vegetables, 1/3 cup pasta sauce, 1/2 cup pasta

PREP TIME: 15 minutes

COOKING TIME: 20 minutes

The cooking method in this quick and easy one-pot meal keeps the pork tenderloin juicy and tender. Smoked paprika gives a smoky flavor to the dish. Half the pork is used for this dinner. The remaining half is used for Tuesday night's dinner.

HELPFUL HINTS:

- Look for trimmed green beans in the produce section to cut down on preparation time.
- Smoked paprika can be found in the spice section of the supermarket.

COUNTDOWN:

- Assemble ingredients.
- Complete recipe.

PORK AND MUSHROOM SKILLET SUPPER

1 1/2 pounds pork tenderloin
2 tablespoons smoked paprika
1 tablespoon olive oil
1/2 teaspoon salt
1/2 teaspoon freshly ground black pepper
1 pound sliced baby bello mushrooms (about 6 cups)
2 cups frozen chopped green bell pepper
1 cup frozen chopped onion
2 teaspoons minced garlic
1 1/2 cups low-sodium, no-sugar-added pasta sauce*
2 cups water
6 ounces fresh angel hair pasta
1/2 pound green beans, trimmed and cut into 2-inch pieces (about 2 cups)
1 cup chopped cilantro

**Look for low-sodium, no-sugar-added pasta sauce containing per 1/2 cup: 112 calories, 3.5 g fat, 17.7 g carbohydrate, 39 mg sodium.*

1. Remove visible fat from pork and cut into 1-inch cubes. Toss in smoked paprika, making sure all sides of meat are coated.

2. Heat olive oil in a large nonstick skillet over medium-high heat. Add pork and brown 3 minutes, turning to brown all sides. Add salt and pepper. Remove pork to a plate.

3. Add the mushrooms, bell pepper, onion, and garlic to the skillet. Sauté 3 minutes.

4. Add the pasta sauce, water, angel hair pasta, and green beans. Spread the pasta throughout the pan to evenly distribute it. Bring to a boil and cook 3 minutes.

5. Return pork to the skillet to warm 1 minute, stirring to combine it with the other ingredients. Sprinkle cilantro on top and serve.

COST OF MEAL PER PERSON

$4.87

PER SERVING

CHOICES/EXCHANGES
3 starch, 2 nonstarchy vegetable, 5 lean protein

Total Calories 510
Total Fat 10 g
Saturated Fat 2.2 g
Monounsaturated Fat 3.5 g
Trans Fat 0.0 g
Cholesterol 110 mg
Sodium 430 mg
Potassium 1780 mg
Total Carbohydrate 56 g
Fiber 8 g
Sugars 14 g
Protein 49 g
Phosphorus 690 mg

MONDAY NIGHT

SALMON BURGERS WITH SAUTÉED BROCCOLI RAAB

SERVES: 4
SERVING SIZE: 3 1/2 ounces salmon, 2 3/4 cups vegetables, 5 tablespoons bread crumbs, 1 3/4 tablespoons topping, 2 ounces whole-wheat roll, 2 teaspoons oil
PREP TIME: 15 minutes
COOKING TIME: 40 minutes

Add variety to your burger repertoire with these juicy salmon burgers. One and a quarter pounds of salmon is used for this dinner. The remainder of the salmon is used for Wednesday night's dinner.

HELPFUL HINTS:

- Any type of hot pepper jelly can be used.
- Ask for the skin to be removed from the salmon when you buy it.
- If a food processor is not available, the salmon can be chopped with a knife on a cutting board. Its soft flesh makes it easy to chop.
- A quick way to chop scallions is to snip them with a scissors.

COUNTDOWN:

- Preheat broiler or toaster oven for hamburger rolls.
- Prepare salmon burger.
- Cook burgers and hamburger buns.
- Make broccoli raab.

SALMON BURGERS

4 tablespoons reduced-fat mayonnaise
3 tablespoons sweet pickle relish
2 cups frozen chopped onion
2 cups frozen chopped green bell pepper
1 1/4 pounds salmon fillets (wild caught), skin removed
1 1/4 cups whole-wheat bread crumbs
1 egg white
1/4 teaspoon salt
1/2 teaspoon freshly ground black pepper
Olive oil spray
4 whole-wheat hamburger rolls (2 ounces each)
2 small tomatoes, sliced

1. Preheat broiler or toaster oven.

2. Mix mayonnaise and pickle relish together in a small bowl and set aside.

3. Defrost onion and green pepper in a microwave oven for 30 seconds.

4. Remove fat or dark meat from the salmon. Cut into 2-inch cubes and place in food processor. Add the onion, green bell pepper, bread crumbs, and egg white. Add salt and pepper. Chop all together. (Or you can chop and combine all ingredients by hand.) Remove from processor and form into 4 patties about 4 inches in diameter and 1 inch thick each.

5. Heat a large nonstick skillet over medium-high heat and spray with olive oil spray. Carefully lift the burgers with a large spatula and add them to the skillet. Brown burgers on one side, about 1 minute. Lower heat to medium-low and cook 4 minutes. Turn burgers and cook another 3 minutes.

6. Split hamburger rolls in half and toast for a few minutes under the broiler or in a toaster oven, until golden. To serve, place burgers on the bottom half of the hamburger rolls and spread mayonnaise mixture over the burgers. Add the tomato slices on top of the sauce and close the rolls.

SAUTÉED BROCCOLI RAAB

1 pound broccoli raab
2 tablespoons olive oil
2 teaspoons minced garlic

1. Cut off thick broccoli raab stems and discard, leaving the tender part and head.

2. Heat oil in a large skillet over medium-high heat and add the broccoli raab. Toss to make sure all sides are cooking. Sauté 5 minutes. Add the garlic and sauté 5 more minutes.

COST OF MEAL PER PERSON
$4.59

PER SERVING

CHOICES/EXCHANGES
3 starch, 2 nonstarchy vegetable, 4 lean protein, 3 1/2 fat

Total Calories 630
Total Fat 27 g
Saturated Fat 4.0 g
Monounsaturated Fat 9.4 g
Trans Fat 0.0 g
Cholesterol 80 mg
Sodium 640 mg
Potassium 1500 mg
Total Carbohydrate 57 g
Fiber 11 g
Sugars 15 g
Protein 39 g
Phosphorus 590 mg

SDAY NIGHT

GREEK GYRO SANDWICH WITH TZATZIKI SAUCE

SERVES: 4
SERVING SIZE: 5 ounces pork tenderloin, 1/2 teaspoon oil, 1 (6-inch) whole-wheat pita bread, 3/4 cup vegetables, 1/2 cup sauce
PREP TIME: 20 minutes
COOKING TIME: 30 minutes

Gyros (pronounced *yeero*) are pita bread sandwiches filled with meat, lettuce, tomatoes, and tzatziki sauce. Tzatziki is a yogurt-based sauce with cucumbers and spices. It also makes a great vegetable dip.

HELPFUL HINTS:

- One teaspoon dried dill can be used instead of fresh.
- Lemon juice is used in the marinade and tzatziki sauce. Squeeze at one time and divide accordingly.
- To seed a cucumber, peel it and cut it into quarters lengthwise and cut out the seeds.
- Minced garlic can be found in the produce section of the market.

COUNTDOWN:

- Marinate meat.
- Prepare remaining ingredients.
- Make tzatziki sauce.
- Cook meat.
- Assemble sandwich.

GREEK GYRO SANDWICH WITH TZATZIKI SAUCE

1 1/2 pounds pork tenderloin
1 cup red wine
5 teaspoons lemon juice, divided
6 teaspoons minced garlic, divided
2 teaspoons dried oregano
2 teaspoons olive oil
1/4 teaspoon salt
1/2 teaspoon freshly ground black pepper
1 cup peeled, seeded, and diced cucumber
1 cup plain, nonfat yogurt
1 tablespoon fresh chopped dill
4 (6-inch) whole-wheat pita breads
1 cup diced fresh tomatoes
2 cups shredded lettuce

1. Remove visible fat from meat and cut into strips about 2 inches long and 1/2 inch wide.

2. Mix the red wine, 4 teaspoons lemon juice, 4 teaspoons garlic, and oregano together in a bowl or self-seal plastic bag. Add the meat and let marinate 10 minutes while preparing the other ingredients.

3. Heat oil in a large nonstick skillet over high heat. Remove the meat from the marinade and sauté 3 minutes for medium doneness, turning the meat to make sure all sides are browned. Add salt and pepper. Remove to a plate.

4. Mix cucumber, yogurt, remaining garlic, dill, and remaining lemon juice together to make tzatziki sauce. Set aside.

5. Warm the pita breads in an oven or toaster oven for 2–3 minutes.

6. Cut pita breads in half, open the pockets and place on a serving plate. Place the meat, tomatoes, lettuce, and tzatziki in separate bowls or on a serving plate so that people can help themselves. Or, if you prefer, fill the pita breads with meat, lettuce, tomatoes, and tzatziki and serve them on individual plates. If you have leftover fillings, serve them on the side.

COST OF MEAL
PER PERSON

$4.39

PER SERVING

CHOICES/EXCHANGES
2 starch, 1/2 carbohydrate,
1 nonstarchy vegetable,
5 lean protein

Total Calories 460
Total Fat 8 g
Saturated Fat 1.9 g
Monounsaturated Fat 2.7 g
Trans Fat 0.0 g
Cholesterol 110 mg
Sodium 560 mg
Potassium 1205 mg
Total Carbohydrate 46 g
Fiber 6 g
Sugars 7 g
Protein 46 g
Phosphorus 640 mg

WEDNESDAY NIGHT

SALMON CHOWDER

SERVES: 4
SERVING SIZE: 5 ounces salmon,
1 1/2 cups vegetables and herbs,
1 1/2 cups potatoes, 1 1/2 cups soup,
1 1/2 tablespoons mustard cream
PREP TIME: 20 minutes
COOKING TIME: 25 minutes

Salmon, fresh herbs, and a tangy mustard cream make a comforting chowder the whole family will enjoy.

HELPFUL HINTS:

- Ask for the skin to be removed from the salmon when you buy it.
- To save preparation time, you can slice all of the vegetables in a food processor.
- A quick way to chop chives is to cut them with a scissors.

COUNTDOWN:

- Prepare all ingredients.
- Make chowder.

SALMON CHOWDER

Olive oil spray
2 cups sliced onion
1 cup sliced celery
1 cup sliced carrots
2 pounds washed and cubed russet or Idaho potato about 6 cups cubes)
3 cups fat-free, no-salt-added chicken broth
3 cups water
1 1/2 pounds salmon fillets (wild caught)
1/2 cup fresh thyme
OR 2 tablespoons dried thyme
2 tablespoons Dijon mustard
1/4 cup whipping cream
1/4 teaspoon salt
1/2 teaspoon freshly ground black pepper
1/2 cup chopped fresh chives
OR 2 tablespoons freeze-dried chives

1. Heat a large nonstick saucepan over medium-high heat and spray with olive oil spray.

2. Add onion, celery, and carrots to the saucepan. Sauté 5 minutes.

3. Add potato cubes to saucepan along with chicken broth and water. Raise heat to high, cover and boil 10 minutes.

4. While potatoes cook, rinse fish, pat dry, and cut into 2-inch pieces. Reduce heat to low and add salmon and thyme to the saucepan. Stir. Simmer gently for 5 minutes or until salmon turns pink. Do not boil.

5. Remove saucepan from heat. Mix mustard and cream together in a bowl and stir into the soup. Add salt and pepper. Divide among 4 large soup bowls and sprinkle chives on top.

COST OF MEAL
PER PERSON

$5.84

PER SERVING

CHOICES/EXCHANGES
3 starch, 1 nonstarchy vegetable, 5 lean protein, 1 fat

Total Calories 530
Total Fat 19 g
Saturated Fat 5.4 g
Monounsaturated Fat 6.5 g
Trans Fat 0.0 g
Cholesterol 115 mg
Sodium 500 mg
Potassium 2385 mg
Total Carbohydrate 48 g
Fiber 7 g
Sugars 8 g
Protein 44 g
Phosphorus 635 mg

THURSDAY NIGHT
TURKEY POT PIE

SERVES: 4
SERVING SIZE: 5 ounces turkey tenderloin, 1/2 tablespoon oil, 1 tablespoon flour, 2 3/4 cups vegetables, 3/4 biscuit (1 1/2 ounces)
PREP TIME: 15 minutes
COOKING TIME: 40 minutes

Pot pies are warm, inviting, and make a great family meal. Topping it with refrigerated biscuit dough gives a golden crust that's easy to prepare. Smoked paprika gives the pie a comforting, smoky touch.

The turkey here is cooked for both tonight and Saturday; half is saved for Saturday night's Turkey Hash.

HELPFUL HINTS:

- Any type of sliced mushrooms can be used.
- Smoked paprika can be found in the spice section of the market.
- Frozen diced onion and green bell pepper are used to cut down on preparation time. Fresh can be used instead of frozen.

COUNTDOWN:

- Preheat oven to 400°F.
- Prepare pie ingredients.
- Make pie.

TURKEY POT PIE

3 pounds turkey tenderloin (half saved for Saturday's dinner)
3 tablespoons canola oil, divided
3 tablespoons smoked paprika
3 cups frozen diced onion
3 cups frozen diced green bell pepper
3 cups sliced baby bello mushrooms
4 tablespoons flour
1 cup fat-free, no-salt-added chicken broth
3 tablespoons fresh tarragon OR 3 teaspoons dried tarragon
1 cup frozen peas
1 cup canned, sliced sweet pimentos
1/2 teaspoon freshly ground black pepper
3 pieces ready-to-cook refrigerated biscuit dough (6 ounces)

KITCHEN COOKWARE:

Deep-dish ovenproof bowl measuring about 10 inches wide and 4 inches deep

1. Preheat oven to 400°F.

2. Cut turkey tenderloin into 1/2-inch pieces. Heat 2 tablespoons of the oil in a large nonstick skillet over medium-high heat. Sprinkle turkey tenderloin with smoked paprika and toss to make sure all the turkey is coated. Add to the skillet. Sauté 5 minutes or until turkey is cooked, stirring to make sure all sides are browned. A meat thermometer inserted into turkey should read 165°F.

3. Remove half the turkey to a bowl, cover, and refrigerate for Saturday night's dinner. Remove the remaining turkey to a deep ovenproof dish.

4. Add the remaining 1 tablespoon oil to the skillet and add the onion, green pepper, and mushrooms. Sauté 5 minutes. Add the flour and mix it with the onion, pepper, and mushrooms. Add the chicken broth. Simmer to thicken, about 1 minute. Mix the tarragon, peas, and pimentos into the sauce. Add pepper. Pour the sauce over the turkey and mix well.

5. Slice the pre-made biscuits in half horizontally so they will be half as thick. Place them over the turkey and vegetables and stretch them to cover the top. Bake for 15 minutes. The biscuits will rise and turn a golden brown. Serve immediately.

COST OF MEAL PER PERSON

$5.18

PER SERVING

CHOICES/EXCHANGES
2 1/2 starch, 2 nonstarchy vegetable, 5 lean protein

Total Calories 480
Total Fat 12 g
Saturated Fat 2.2 g
Monounsaturated Fat 4.8 g
Trans Fat 0.0 g
Cholesterol 90 mg
Sodium 610 mg
Potassium 1245 mg
Total Carbohydrate 48 g
Fiber 7 g
Sugars 14 g
Protein 50 g
Phosphorus 680 mg

FRIDAY NIGHT

RICOTTA SOUFFLÉ WITH TOMATO BRUSCHETTA

SERVES: 4

SERVING SIZE: 2 3/4 cups vegetables,
1 1/2 teaspoons oil,
5 tablespoons bread crumb topping,
1/2 cup nonfat ricotta, 1/4 egg, 1/2 egg white,
2 slices whole-wheat bread

PREP TIME: 20 minutes

COOKING TIME: 40 minutes

Sautéed vegetables mixed with ricotta cheese and topped with bread crumbs make this an unusual soufflé. The zucchini and carrots are grated and the mushrooms and onions are sliced, providing a variety of textures.

HELPFUL HINTS:

- To save preparation time, grate the zucchini and carrots in a food processor. If you don't have a shredding blade, the carrots and zucchini can be thinly sliced instead of grated.

COUNTDOWN:

- Preheat oven to 400°F.
- Make soufflé.
- While soufflé bakes, prepare bruschetta topping.
- Toast bread slices for bruschetta in the oven for a few minutes just before the soufflé is finished cooking.

RICOTTA SOUFFLÉ

4 teaspoons canola oil
2 cups grated zucchini
2 cups grated carrots
3 cups sliced button mushrooms
1 cup sliced red onion
1 cup chopped fresh basil
1 1/2 cups plain whole-wheat bread crumbs
1/4 teaspoon salt
1/2 teaspoon freshly ground black pepper
2 cups nonfat ricotta cheese
1 large whole egg
2 egg whites

1. Preheat oven to 400°F.

2. Heat oil in a large nonstick skillet over medium heat. Add zucchini, carrots, mushrooms, and onion. Cover with a lid and cook 5 minutes.

3. Meanwhile, in a small bowl, mix basil with bread crumbs and add salt and pepper. Set aside.

4. Remove vegetables from heat, spoon into a 10 × 8-inch ovenproof dish or lasagna dish and spread out to cool.

5. Mix the ricotta cheese and eggs together. Then combine the cheese mixture with the vegetables and spread evenly in the pan. Sprinkle bread crumb mixture on top. Bake 15 minutes. Then cover with foil to prevent the bread crumbs from burning and continue to bake 10 minutes.

6. Remove from oven and serve with bruschetta.

TOMATO BRUSCHETTA

8 slices whole-wheat baguette (6 ounces)
1 medium clove garlic
2 cups diced fresh tomatoes
2 teaspoons canola oil
1/2 teaspoon freshly ground black pepper

1. Line a baking tray with foil. Place baguette slices on the tray and toast in oven with the soufflé until golden, about 3–4 minutes.

2. Remove from oven. Cut garlic clove in half and rub cut halves over the toasted bread.

3. In a medium-size bowl, toss diced tomato and olive oil together. Add salt and pepper. Spoon mixture over bread and serve.

COST OF MEAL
PER PERSON
$2.48

PER SERVING

CHOICES/EXCHANGES
3 starch, 2 nonstarchy vegetable, 2 lean protein, 1 fat

Total Calories 420
Total Fat 11 g
Saturated Fat 1.5 g
Monounsaturated Fat 5.3 g
Trans Fat 0.0 g
Cholesterol 45 mg
Sodium 590 mg
Potassium 1070 mg
Total Carbohydrate 55 g
Fiber 8 g
Sugars 15 g
Protein 23 g
Phosphorus 585 mg

SATURDAY NIGHT
TURKEY HASH

SERVES: 4
SERVING SIZE: 5 ounces turkey, 3/4 cup vegetables, 1/2 cup sweet potatoes, 3/4 tablespoon oil, 1/4 cup reduced-fat cheese, 1/4 cup cranberry sauce
PREP TIME: 15 minutes
COOKING TIME: 15 minutes

Turkey, cranberry sauce, vegetables, and sweet potatoes combine to make this tasty meal. It's a one-pot dinner! It uses the cooked turkey reserved from Thursday night's meal, so it's easy to prepare.

HELPFUL HINTS:

- Any type of boneless, skinless poultry can be used for this recipe.
- Vegetables can be sliced in the food processor.
- Minced garlic can be found in the produce section of the market.

COUNTDOWN:

- Prepare ingredients.
- Microwave the potatoes.
- Make the hash.

TURKEY HASH

2 cups peeled and chopped sweet potatoes (1/2-inch pieces)
2 tablespoons canola oil
1 1/2 cups sliced onion
2 cups sliced celery
2 teaspoons minced garlic
1 1/2 pounds cooked turkey (saved from Thursday night)
1 1/3 cups whole berry cranberry sauce
1/2 cup water
1/4 teaspoon salt
1/2 teaspoon freshly ground black pepper
1 cup shredded, reduced-fat Monterey Jack cheese

1. Place potatoes in a bowl and microwave on high 3 minutes.

2. Heat the oil in a large nonstick skillet over medium-high heat. Add the potatoes, onion, celery, and garlic. Sauté 5 minutes.

3. Add the turkey and sauté 2 minutes. Add cranberry sauce and water. Sauté 2 minutes. Add salt and pepper.

4. Sprinkle cheese on top and cover with a lid. Cook 2 minutes or until cheese melts, then serve.

COST OF MEAL
PER PERSON

$4.30

PER SERVING

CHOICES/EXCHANGES
1 starch, 2 1/2 carbohydrate,
1 nonstarchy vegetable,
6 lean protein, 1 fat

Total Calories 580
Total Fat 18 g
Saturated Fat 4.5 g
Monounsaturated Fat 6.9 g
Trans Fat 0.0 g
Cholesterol 110 mg
Sodium 580 mg
Potassium 950 mg
Total Carbohydrate 59 g
Fiber 5 g
Sugars 35 g
Protein 50 g
Phosphorus 545 mg

INDEX

D

E

F

G

H

J

K

L

M